Managing for
Peak Performance

Managing for Peak Performance

A Guide to the Power (and Pitfalls) of Personal Style

Alan Weiss

1817

Harper & Row, Publishers, New York

BALLINGER DIVISION

Grand Rapids, Philadelphia, St. Louis, San Francisco
London, Singapore, Sydney, Tokyo, Toronto

International Standard Book Number: O-88730-337-4

Library of Congress Catalog Card Number: 89-35086

Printed in the United States of America

Library of Congress Cataloging-in-Publication Data

Weiss, Alan Jay, 1946–
    Managing for peak performance: a guide to the power (and pitfalls) of personal style / Alan Weiss.
        p.   cm.
    Includes index.
    ISBN 0-88730-337-4
    1. Personnel management.   2. Achievement motivation.
3. Performance.   4. Organizational behavior.   I. Title.
HF5549.W43116   1989
658.4'09—dc20   89-35086
                                                        CIP

89 90 91 92 HC 9 8 7 6 5 4 3 2 1

For Maria . . .
. . . as is everything

Contents

Acknowledgments

I wish to acknowledge the cooperation and support of the more than 100 clients of Summit Consulting Group who contributed—directly and indirectly—to this work. The approaches in this book are not theoretical models waiting to be tested in the workplace, but management models constructed over the course of sixteen years of on-site observations and interventions. Specifically, I am grateful to our professional colleagues at Merck & Co., Inc., Bally's Grand Hotel, American Press Institute, Atlantic Electric Company, and Decision Processes International for their valuable openness and trust.

Sincere thanks also to Judy Zimmer for her editorial assistance, and to Marjorie Richman, my editor, who has expertly guided me through our second book together.

Introduction:
The Keys to Performance and Fulfillment

Not long ago, I found myself in the challenging and difficult position of addressing seventy-five bank presidents and top quality officers on techniques to achieve superior performance in their organizations. My initial instructions were terrifyingly simple: just teach senior management the basic steps necessary to sustain high levels of motivation throughout the ranks of middle management.

Those instructions were also *deceptively* simple. I didn't fall off a turnip truck yesterday, and I've heard too many speakers, consultants, and line managers talk about "motivation" as if it were a single technique that improves performance. It's not. In the first place, performers have to motivate themselves, because no one else can. Management can *create the conditions* under which people will tend to become motivated, but motivation remains an intrinsic and private affair. Second, those conditions will only come about if management acts competently in three key areas: finding the right person, structuring the position correctly, and only then establishing the proper mechanisms to ensure superior performance.

The right *person* is the most critical factor of all. The immutable fact is that you can't turn goats into eagles. Giving the goat a specially tailored, $10,000 set of training wings doesn't make it an eagle—just an uncomfortable goat that still can't fly and has cost you a bundle. Now, goats are noble animals, and there are excellent pursuits for them—jobs that eagles will never do. But goats can't fly, and investing time and energy in hoping they will is akin to leaving the landing lights on for Amelia Earhart.

Hiring the right people is, of course, the first step managers take toward staffing their organizations for success, yet selection is one of management's most abused and taken-for-granted responsibilities. Good selection can save a huge amount of money down the road. Poor selection will inevitably cost you, no matter how good the rest of your systems and procedures are. Yet few managers are well trained or well equipped to make decisions about hiring, promotion, transfer, and so forth, and few organizations do much to help them. Here's an observation from a study on motivation by Professor Barry Staw of the University of California School of Business Administration at Berkeley:

> High morale is most easily achieved when the company hires motivated people in the first place. Many company programs aimed at enhancing worker happiness and productivity fail because some employees have personalities that simply don't respond to the efforts. Attitudes toward work are largely shaped by emotional makeup, and workers with negative attitudes about themselves may be difficult to motivate.[1]

Before being hired, the "right person" already manifests the behaviors that are essential to successful performance. According to a *Fortune* magazine poll (1987–1989) of CEOs, Merck & Co., Inc., was "America's most admired company" for the previous three years. In a project for Merck, we found that the company doesn't need to spend much time or energy inculcating new employees with the organization's values because it does an excellent job of attracting people who already hold those values. Moreover, its management practices exemplify those values on a daily basis. It's no accident that the top companies are the ones that undertake self-scrutiny.

The right *position* means that the structure provides the appropriate prerogatives, support systems, resources, and so on for the right *person* to do the job. A great batter can't hit the ball if he's not permitted to get close to the plate. A manager can't meet commitments to people without the resources and authority required to do so.

And the right performance is attained by enabling the right *people* in the right *positions* to regularly assess their work. Performance goals should be adjusted according to the gratification inherent in achieving personal objectives and satisfying personal values, not according to arbitrary management fiat or—worst of all—policies created in reaction to misdeeds elsewhere. (Such attempts almost always punish the innocent and ignore those who are really at fault.) Employees should share in the setting of their performance goals.

Motivation itself is no simple matter, and it is only one element of good performance. But motivation can be managed effectively when the components of good performance are understood. The right person is one who not only can but *wants* to do the job; the right position is a job that he or she can do; and the right performance comes with the right person in the right position given the opportunity to do the desired job. This approach to performance has implications for hiring, training, reward systems, management practices, and so forth. But that's the challenge of thinking beyond a simple view of motivation and, instead, resolving to manage performance.

In an age when middle management ranks are thinning and managers at all levels are under increasingly competitive pressures, answering the question, "Why do managers fail?" becomes essential.

Of the five causes listed below, assign a number to each indicating its priority as a contributor to manager failure:

1. Inability to get along with others ___ .
2. Failure to adapt one's style __.
3. The "me only" syndrome (alienating others) __.
4. Fear of action __.
5. Inability to rebound __.

Respondents to a survey of 191 top executives conducted by the Center for Creative Leadership (CCL) cited these causes in the order they appear.[2] That is, the top three causes of management failure *are all behaviorally and interpersonally based,* according to this poll. But in my work with hundreds of organizations in four countries, I've consistently found this result, no matter who the poll-takers or the respondents are.

This survey cites the "inability to get along" as the most crucial flaw to recognize and remedy. Apparently, respondents often view conflict as inherently bad, rather than as an opportunity to air legitimate differences. You can seldom "damn the torpedoes" with people, no matter who you are. To be successful, you must adapt to others. (One of my career counseling clients, exemplifying the inevitable result of a failure to adapt, remarked to me that he left his prior position because of his boss's illness. "Whenever the boss saw me, he got sick.")

The study states that "the inability to adapt to change is the fatal flaw of the fast-tracker who clings to a once-successful management style . . . long after it stops producing results." One respondent states, "The traits my boss once found endearing in me—my outspokenness, my strong opinions, my negotiating toughness—became annoying and unacceptable" when the organization's entrepreneurial direction was abandoned. She suddenly found herself serving as an administrator , not an adventurer. No successful manager assumes that a given style will *always* be effective, despite changing conditions, people, and environments. Compatibility of a person and a job is situational.

"Managers are rarely dismissed because of poor performance," concludes another study. "Dismissal usually is the result of clashes with superiors caused by: incompatible personalities and/or disagreement about style."[3]

Finally, the CCL study cites the narcissists who alienate others through self-centeredness. (I believe it was Woody Allen who said that a narcissist is someone who's better looking than you are.) These are managers who aren't able to adjust to participative, team-oriented approaches, unless the spotlight remains focused on them. But how many of these managers failing for this reason are being mislabeled "narcissistic" when in fact they are failing because they don't know *what* behaviors are required, or *how* to acquire them?

Several years ago, a management training client asked Summit Consulting Group to investigate the low productivity of his sales force. He wanted to know whether he should implement a training program that his director of human resources wanted or secure the services of an outside "motivational speaker" strongly recommended by a business associate.

We found a sales force composed of people who were extremely analytical and precise. They were very consistent and unassertive and tended to *refrain* from initiating social contact. Their main source of gratification was pleasing their superiors, to the point of telling them what they thought their superiors wanted to hear. They were nice people, intelligent people, talented people, trustworthy people—but they certainly weren't *sales*people. And no amount of training, inspiration, witch's brew, or alchemy would make them so.

They were hired by the vice president of administration—a careful, numbers-oriented, thorough individual who happened to believe that the best possible candidates for any job were those cut from familiar cloth. Thus, a battalion of accountants was hired to operate the sales guns. Small wonder that the guns kept misfiring.

Our advice to that client and others has led to this book. An understanding of behavior and its relationship to performance is essential to every manager who is charged with working with others to achieve organizational goals. There are clear, logical, and predictive factors that tell us why some people follow through diligently while others are perpetually late; why some can freeze you with their tone of voice while others encourage rapport; why some seek acceptance while others enjoy the role of maverick.

It is simply untrue that anyone can do anything if properly inspired. No silly craze, whether rappeling down mountains or trodding hot coals, will alter this reality, though such fads might come in handy for those climbing mountains during forest fires. A passion for excellence must be predicated on a search for competence.

Most of *can* do many things. But the key questions are: for how long, and at what price? Being able to do something is not the same as *wanting* to do something. (Think about cutting the grass or cleaning the kitchen.) Just because an individual can do something does not guarantee that the performance will be sustained. Consequently, how can a manager predict performance—his or her own or that of others—with any reliability?

An individual's past success is not an indicator of future success. Yet, as you read this, legions of managers throughout the country are promoting the best salespeople to sales manager, the best underwriters to underwriting manager, and the best tellers to head teller. All of them are courting a better than 50/50 chance of removing a good performer and creating a lousy manager. How *do* you make decisions about promotion, selection, and personal career paths, especially in an age in which stress is rapidly becoming the primary workplace disability? It is no accident that all-star players are seldom effective managers, or that great managers were seldom star players.

As in so many cases, the keys to performance, productivity, and personal fulfillment are based in common sense. However, we need to view the world and our own behavior in a manner that is different from that which has been inculcated into us all. This book provides that different view—a view of personal success and organizational achievement, based on practical, methodical approaches to people decisions we all have to make.

Notes

1. Barry Staw, cited in Alan Weiss, "Willingness is Not Enough," *Training News* (August 1987): 14.
2. As cited in *Wall Street Journal*, 2 May 1988.
3. Richard Gould, *Sacked: Why Good People Get Fired* (New York: John Wiley & Sons, 1986).

1

Why We Do
the Things We Do:
The Role of
Behavior in Our Work

Natural ability without education has oftener raised
people to glory and virtue, than education without
natural ability.
—Cicero

When I was in grade school, I was told frequently by people I
respected that I ought to be a lawyer. "You speak so well," said
my parents. "You have an excellent command of information,"
said my teachers. "Oh, let's give it up—Weiss is gonna argue,"
said my friends. And so, like the ancient mariner's big bird, the
legal profession began to pursue me through all kinds of waters.

In high school, teachers and counselors steered me toward an
attorney's preparation. My speaking and writing abilities were
cited as examples of why I was cut out to be a lawyer. (It was
years later that I realized that these and other talents represented
any number of possibilities. But at the time, everything I did was
caught in the centripetal force of *the law*.)

No one in my family had ever attended college, much less been
a lawyer. It seemed like *all* of us were becoming lawyers—I was
simply the implementer. Everyone around me was intoning "pre-
law" as a kind of ritualistic chant. Finally, in my senior year of
college, I was not only accepted by an excellent law school, but
I won a full scholarship. Nearly everyone was ecstatic. In fact,
I was the lone holdout.

During that summer, I came to a visceral conclusion. It was not based on any argument I could rationally present, and I certainly had no process at the time to understand the roots of my discomfort. But I knew one thing as sure as I knew that it was right to root for the Dodgers: *I didn't want to be a lawyer!*

The epilogue to this story is that I went to see the law school dean of admissions and told her of my decision so that someone else could receive the scholarship. Her response was classic: "Are you crazy?! You ought to be a lawyer!" I ran out of there as fast as I could and haven't looked back since.

Friends, how many people are drilling on your teeth who really don't want to be dentists?

Self-Perception and Behavior

Our perceptions about ourselves and what we "should" be are formed very early. Few of us have the conscious opportunity to periodically examine these perceptions to check their validity. They pile up, like dusty mementos in the attic, without scrutiny or reassessment. Yet unlike the unseen relics stored in fading boxes, these perceptions color the way we think about ourselves and our consequent behaviors and actions. We choose careers and our lifework because of what our parents did, what friends told us, or what enemies imposed upon us. And we choose to act in certain ways for all the wrong reasons—because of financial pressure, peer pressure, expectation pressure, and a myriad of other pressures. In other words, we are *reacting*—rather than *acting* in a comfortable manner based on our native abilities and talents.

Our self-perceptions are the critical ingredient in our behavior. This is because perception *is* reality. We act on the basis of what we perceive about ourselves and our environment. There is no empirical yardstick against which we measure the accuracy of these perceptions.

Here's a demonstration of this phenomenon. As honestly as you can, place yourself in this scenario: You are seven years old. In the next room are people who know you well—parents, guardians, friends, teachers—and they are talking about you, although they don't know you're listening. In the spaces below, write five statements they would have made about you at the age of seven. Be as specific as possible. ("He's comfortable meeting new people," "She's awkward on the playground," "She speaks her mind readily," "He doesn't like changes," etc.)

_____ ☐

_____ ☐

_____ ☐

_____ ☐

_____ ☐

Now, in the boxes on the right, check those statements that could still be made about you today. Not everyone has to make them about you; simply check the boxes for the statements you believe are still true about you today.

How many did you check? Most people check at least three, and it's not uncommon to check four or five. It is rare to check one or none. Our perceptions of ourselves are formed very early and very subtly, but they tend to take hold like an epoxy glue.

If Jennifer is told that she is poised and comfortable dealing with people and that she makes an excellent impression standing before a group, she will tend to pursue experiences that draw upon those qualities, or at least will readily accept them. In so doing, she will further develop the abilities that are important in such situations. If Jason, however, is told that he's laughable on the baseball field and that his abilities are well below those of others his age, he may well shy away from baseball, thereby denying himself the opportunity to develop the requisite skills for it. We inadvertently create and suffer through these self-fulfilling prophecies when we allow them to become "facts" and "givens," instead of simply perceptions that may not be grounded in reality.

There have been many classic studies conducted along these lines. For instance, two teachers are given classes of students who, until then, scored identically in their testing and performance. But one teacher was told that class A was remedial, while the other was told class B was advanced. At the end of the test period, sure enough, students in class B received higher grades and better ratings than their otherwise identical colleagues in class A. What was different? Only the *perceptions* of the teachers—yet those perceptions significantly affected the teachers' attitudes, actions, and expectations, as well as the actual "results" achieved by the classes.

Look around you. How significantly are perceptions determining the performance of people within your organization? Of people you manage? What effect do they have on your hiring techniques? On your assessment of results? On how you deal with colleagues and customers? What happens when a new manager assumes command? Typically, he or she is briefed by the incumbent, the boss, or new colleagues. The newcomer might also review personnel records and the inevitable locked-away files. Yet those briefings, records, and files only serve to perpetuate *others'* perceptions for the newcomer. It is our experience that, merely by examining the bases for these perceptions, people can dramatically improve their relationships and the results generated by their staffs. In later chapters, we'll provide examples and techniques for ways to do this on the job. But first, a greater understanding of behavior and the role it plays in working with others is required.

Take a look at the grid below. How many squares do you see? Write the number in the space provided.

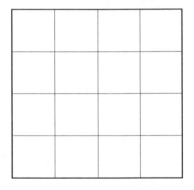

Number of Squares: _____

Seem simple? Perhaps, but the responses usually vary from sixteen to thirty—that's quite a variation! See page 5 for the possibilities.

Now, what's the *right* number of squares? Is it the maximum number that the most detail-conscious person can detect? Nope—the "right" number is the number that *you* see. Perception is reality. If I had asked you to take some particular action connected with these squares, you would have taken that action based on the number of squares you perceived. Just as the teachers of classes A and B took actions based on their perceptions of their students, people all around you are taking action based on their perceptions of you, your colleagues, and the environment. There simply is no "greater reality."

There is a well-cited exercise performed with first-year law students (see, I just can't seem to stay away from the profession).

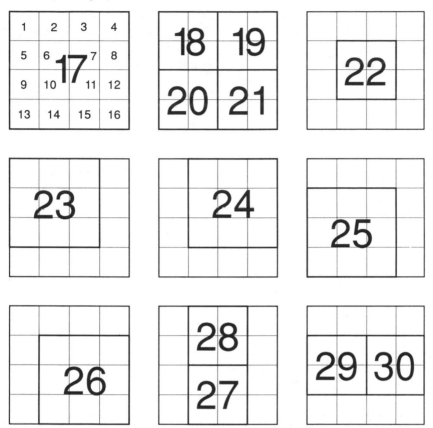

17 (entire grid)

During a class, a gunman rushes in, "shoots" a participant (who's in on the hoax), and dashes out. When canvassed, the class usually can't agree on the assailant's height, eye color, hair color, general physical makeup, or even *gender*. Such is the weakness of "eyewitness" reporting.

Our perceptions, not actual events, often dictate who we believe we saw commit a crime, who's the best candidate for promotion, and what the buyer intends to do after the meeting. Organizationally, we may restructure departments, implement motivational programs, and change marketing approaches based on perceptions that are far afield from reality. This is why external consultants, marketing research firms, and customer focus groups are so widely used as aids in testing organizational perceptions against reality. (One adhesives company president sheepishly told me that he was saved from a costly redesign of his primary production machine only when an outside firm was able to demonstrate that the equipment was operating at 100 percent of its specifications, despite his perception that it was sluggish.)

For those of you who still think that there are absolute answers, and that the squares simply required a "logical" approach, here's one more shot. Now that you know my tricks, this one should be easy.

Which line, A–B or C–D, is closer to you?

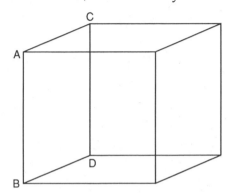

As you can "see," there is no "right," logical answer to this one. Once you've had the opportunity to study the cube, you can see that there are two ways to perceive it, though you may strongly favor one over the other. (Hint: C–D is the left side of the cube's front, and A–B is the rear left.) If a colleague chooses the other, you can at least understand his or her position. Line A–B could be one interpretation of managerial behavior, line C–D another. You perceive A–B as "correct" (nearer you), your colleague C–D. Who's accurate?

For example, a consulting/training firm we worked with discovered that its sales force was averaging 25 percent less revenue than its competitors. Top management's perception, based solely on the opinions of the sales managers, was that the salespeople needed more motivation. This was reinforced by articles the sales managers circulated about the need constantly to motivate the sales force. Consequently, the firm offered two new Cadillacs to the two highest revenue generators.

The result was predictable. The prior year's two top performers won the cars *with precisely the same level of revenue generation they had achieved the prior year.* In other words, they received a $25,000 bonus for the same performance, and the organization spent $50,000 more to get the same performance—the very definition of productivity *decline.*

The sales force's perception was that the organization placed value on doing better than one's colleagues, *not* on exceeding a common performance goal. Consequently, a win/lose environment encouraged salespeople to compete with each other only as long as they could be number one. Management perceived this as a motivation problem (encouraged by sales managers who found it easier to give money away than to manage the system) rather than a systemic problem.

By implementing an uncapped incentive system in which *everyone* could win if sales goals were exceeded, we were able to improve productivity at less net cost than giving away cars. What's often called by critics "poor problem-solving" is often actually a result of taking action based on unshared perceptions.

Self-Test: Understanding Your Own Behavior

The following chapters will tell you how to identify behavioral predispositions and what can be done to successfully manage and motivate people in light of them. But it might be of interest to first understand your own behaviors and predispositions, to test your perceptions about yourself. Normally, this is best done as a formal test, but if you'll allow for the unscientific nature of a self-test, you might wish to invest some time in creating your own behavioral profile.

Remember, we can't guarantee the results will be 100 percent accurate, but our experience is that they're reliable better than 90 percent of the time. And the information generated should provide some insights as you read the remaining chapters with this personal feedback in mind.

First, in the spaces below, write ten adjectives that you believe describe you well—for example, assertive, shy, compassionate, joyful, stern, rigorous, and so forth. Don't ask anyone for help.

_____   _____

_____   _____

_____   _____

_____   _____

_____   _____

Now, check off those words below that you believe really describe you. Check all that apply, being as honest as possible. Move quickly; if you're uncertain, check the word.

SELF-TEST

1___apprehensive	34___bold	67___original
2___dignified	35___trusting	68___appealing to others
3___cautious	36___careful	69___esteemed
4___delightful	37___conforming	70___certain
5___glib	38___fair	71___distinctive
6___doubting	39___crafty	72___wavering
7___dreaming	40___inflexible	73___highly competent
8___easily hurt	41___daring	74___moral
9___emotional	42___exacting	75___modern
10___obliging	43___endearing	76___impulsive
11___fearful	44___demanding	77___exceptional
12___entertaining	45___forgetful	78___independent
13___eager	46___principled	79___nonjudgmental
14___fashionable	47___ill at ease	80___intellectual
15___peculiar	48___polite	81___fortunate
16___nervous	49___opinionated	82___plotting
17___selective	50___friendly	83___practial
18___open	51___progressive	84___fun-loving
19___precise	52___reflective	85___problem-solving
20___sensible	53___genial	86___self-confident
21___regretful	54___tenacious	87___self-controlled
22___graceful	55___sensitive	88___strong-willed
23___unselfish	56___humorous	89___suspicious
24___impassioned	57___jolly	90___well-informed
25___sympathetic	58___loving	91___thin-skinned
26___traditional	59___troubled	92___well-liked
27___solid	60___unshakabie	93___vigorous
28___adult	61___calm	94___civil
29___compassionate	62___helpful	95___hard to excite
30___impartial	63___kindly	96___mild
31___neat	64___proper	97___nonaggressive
32___quiet	65___tolerant	98___self-content
33___unhurried	66___withdrawn	99___uncomplicated

In the scoring key, each of the 99 words has been given a designation of 1, 2, 3, 4, or a dot. For only those words you've checked, find its designation in the scoring key. If it has a dot, ignore it. If it has a number 1 to 4, put a mark in the following tabulation boxes.

SCORING KEY

1_*4*_apprehensive	34_*1*_bold	67_·_original
2_*5*_dignified	35_·_trusting	68_*2*_appealing to others
3_*4*_cautious	36_*1*_careful	69_*5*_esteemed
4_*2*_delightful	37_*4*_conforming	70_*1*_certain
5_·_glib	38_*5*_fair	71_*2*_distinctive
6_*4*_doubting	39_*1*_crafty	72_·_wavering
7_*2*_dreaming	40_·_inflexible	73_*5*_highly competent
8_*4*_easily hurt	41_*1*_daring	74_*5*_moral
9_*2*_emotional	42_*4*_exacting	75_·_modern
10_*5*_obliging	43_*2*_endearing	76_*1*_impulsive
11_*4*_fearful	44_*1*_demanding	77_·_exceptional
12_*2*_entertaining	45_*4*_forgetful	78_*1*_independent
13_·_eager	46_*5*_principled	79_*5*_nonjudgmental
14_*2*_fashionable	47_*4*_ill at ease	80_*1*_intellectual
15_·_peculiar	48_*5*_polite	81_*2*_fortunate
16_*4*_nervous	49_*1*_opinionated	82_·_plotting
17_*5*_selective	50_*2*_friendly	83_*1*_practial
18_*1*_open	51_·_progressive	84_*2*_fun-loving
19_*4*_precise	52_·_reflective	85_*1*_problem-solving
20_*5*_sensible	53_*2*_genial	86_*5*_self-confident
21_*4*_regretful	54_*1*_tenacious	87_*5*_self-controlled
22_*2*_graceful	55_*4*_sensitive	88_*1*_strong-willed
23_*5*_unselfish	56_*2*_humorous	89_*4*_suspicious
24_*2*_impassioned	57_*2*_jolly	90_*5*_well-informed
25_*4*_sympathetic	58_*2*_loving	91_*4*_thin-skinned
26_*4*_traditional	59_*4*_troubled	92_*2*_well-liked
27_*1*_solid	60_*1*_unshakable	93_*1*_vigorous
28_*3*_adult	61_*3*_calm	94_*3*_civil
29_*3*_compassionate	62_*3*_helpful	95_*3*_hard to excite
30_*3*_impartial	63_*3*_kindly	96_*3*_mild
31_*3*_neat	64_*3*_proper	97_*3*_nonaggressive
32_*3*_quiet	65_*3*_tolerant	98_*3*_self-content
33_*3*_unhurried	66_*3*_withdrawn	99_*3*_uncomplicated

1 [_____] 2 [_____] 3 [_____] 4 [_____] 5 [_____]

For example, if you checked word 9, "emotional," put a mark in tabulation box 2. If you checked word 46, "principled," put a mark in tabulation box 5. If you checked word 82, "plotting," do not mark any tabulation box.

Be careful in totaling your scores—even a small error can make a large difference in the feedback. If you have fifteen or fewer total marks in categories 1–5, the feedback may be somewhat less accurate than if you had more marks. But do not go back to create more, or you'll skew the feedback.

Finally, transfer the numbers to the chart below by placing a dot on the appropriate number. Connect the first four points to form a pattern.

1		0 1 2	3 4 5 6 7 8	9 10 11 12 13 14 15	16 17 18	
2		0 1 2 3	4 5 6 7 8 9 10 11 12	13 14 15 16 17 18	
3	0	1 2 3	4 5	6 7	8 9 10	11 12	13 14	15 16 17	18	
4			0 1	2 3	4 5	6 7 8	9 10	11 12 13	14 15	16 17 18
5	0 1	2 3	4 5	6 7	8	9 10	11 12	13 14	15	

For example, if your results were 1:12, 2:8, 3:6, 4:4 and 5:9, your pattern would look like this:

1		0 1 2	3 4 5 6 7 8	9 10 11• 12 13 14 15	16 17 18	
2		0 1 2 3	4 5 6 7• 8 9 10 11 12	13 14 15 16 17 18	
3	0	1 2 3	4 5 •6	7 8 9 10	11 12	13 14	15 16 17	18	
4			0 1	2 3 •4 5	6 7 8	9 10	11 12 13	14 15	16 17 18
5	0 1	2 3	4 5	6 7	8 •9 10	11 12	13 14	15	

You now have a picture of your natural predispositions—those behaviors that, left to your own devices, are most comfortable to you. This is your "home base," or where you naturally prefer to be. We'll now provide a brief summary of the major behavior patterns that emerge from this type of testing. Remember, this is not meant to be scientific or comprehensive, but only to provide some personal feedback that will help you appreciate the following chapters and evaluate your own self-perceptions.

We'll describe eighteen possible profiles, but these are by no means the only ones possible. If yours falls between any two, then you probably exhibit a combination of those traits. Moreover, all behaviors are influenced by factors that can't be fully measured here, factors such as energy, morale, flexibility, and the strength of behavioral predispositions.

Finally, all of us are capable of change, though to varying degrees. There might well be instances in which the behavior indicated by the pattern is not like you at all. The litmus test, though, is whether the profile describes you under normal conditions.

DETAILED AND ACCURATE

This individual . . .

. . . tends to be as accurate and thorough as possible

. . . is very practical in approach

. . . avoids confrontation and controversy

. . . prefers a relatively slow-paced work environment

. . . is compliant and likes to satisfy others

. . . makes decisions reactively and cautiously

. . . seeks help, information, and often, consensus

. . . is prudent and careful

. . . is not impulsive and wants the facts prior to action

. . . appreciates order and procedure

. . . enjoys analyzing data, details, and particulars

. . . is generally hesitant to delegate

. . . tends to have very structured and neat work habits

Words that can describe this individual include:

sensitive	methodical	detail-oriented
polite	mannered	considerate
analytical	prudent	good listener
calm	responsive	controlled
cautious	reactive	responsible

AMIABLE AND COMPLIANT

	low	high
1		
2		
3		
4		

This individual . . .

    . . . makes decisions only when sufficient data is
        present

    . . . is very conscientious and feels strongly about
        obligations

    . . . prefers to be cooperative and to avoid confrontation

    . . . tends to do things "by the book"

    . . . likes to be a team member, but not the leader

    . . . is an objective, reasoned problem solver

    . . . has a strong sense of commitment

    . . . works well with deadlines and completion dates

    . . . can be seen by others as proper in social
        interactions

    . . . can be seen as shy and reserved

    . . . works well with complicated and complex
        information

    . . . usually opts for minimum risk

    . . . doesn't like to work faster than he or she prefers

    . . . is often the stereotypical "organization person"

Words that can describe this individual include:

methodical	compliant	formal
accurate	cautious	reserved
calm	modest	self-effacing
sensitive	vulnerable	data-oriented

PATIENT

This individual . . .

- . . . likes to follow precedent, procedure, and respected people
- . . . is a careful planner and decision maker
- . . . does not readily accept change
- . . . is very reliable with delegated work
- . . . likes to please those in authority
- . . . tends to be compliant
- . . . is usually somewhat sensitive to criticism
- . . . prefers harmonious relationships and acceptance by others
- . . . tends to be contented with the status quo
- . . . does not usually display emotion
- . . . performs best with structure and clear instructions
- . . . likes to be a team member, but not the leader
- . . . is loyal to friends and family

Words that can describe this individual include:

relaxed	amiable	supportive
patient	cautious	mild-mannered
serene	happy	trustworthy
positive	reliable	routine-oriented

SOCIAL AND POLITICAL

	low	high
1		
2		
3		
4		

This individual . . .

> . . . prefers people interactions

> . . . initiates social contacts and friendships

> . . . requires approval from peers and superiors

> . . . prefers to work according to systems and procedures

> . . . is generally cheerful, optimistic, and polite

> . . . is flexible working with different personalities

> . . . desires to be perceived as supportive and cooperative

> . . . tends to become involved in charitable work and causes

> . . . tries to avoid confrontation, friction, and unpleasantness

> . . . establishes influential friends and acquaintances

> . . . is sincerely concerned about others

> . . . develops a poised, suave style

> . . . is usually politically aware and shrewd

> . . . is consistently sensitive in dealing with others

Words that can describe this individual include:

friendly	polite	optimistic
verbal	energetic	supportive of others
happy	cooperative	tolerant
charmer		likable

FRIENDLY

This individual . . .

    . . . is a "natural" and an initiator with others

    . . . usually has a good, nonthreatening sense of humor

    . . . prefers to accomplish objectives through and with others

    . . . sincerely enjoys social interaction

    . . . tends to avoid risk

    . . . appreciates manners, civility, and suavity

    . . . is genuinely likable and liked by most people

    . . . is generally seen as pleasant

    . . . places high value on relationships

    . . . can have difficulty in fairly evaluating others

    . . . establishes relationships readily

    . . . can put even strangers quickly at ease

Words that can describe this individual include:

optimistic	cordial	suave
amenable	flexible	cheerful
vivacious	extroverted	social
pleasing	nice	calm

SERVICE-ORIENTED

low		high
1		
2		
3		
4		

This individual . . .

> . . . is outspoken and states strong positions

> . . . prefers a cordial work environment

> . . . enjoys being supportive of others

> . . . is generally positive about others

> . . . relies easily on others

> . . . can be discouraged when others don't meet commitments

> . . . is very approachable, even for strangers

> . . . can readily "make talk" about almost anything with anyone

> . . . can be seen as a good listener

> . . . is calm and collected, even in crisis situations

> . . . prefers to be part of a team

> . . . works best at an unhurried pace

> . . . can be very stubborn when disagreeing with policy/systems

Words that can describe this individual include:

friendly	calm	sincere
focused	likable	mild-mannered
patient	supportive	approachable
interested	humorous	confident

THOROUGH AND ACCURATE

This individual . . .

   . . . plans and organizes with great care

   . . . prefers to act in a low-profile, nonthreatening manner

   . . . tends to control the environment and issue when risk is minimized

   . . . tries to conform to group pressures and norms

   . . . tries to meet others' expectations

   . . . generally avoids risk unless success is almost guaranteed

   . . . can be seen as a nitpicker

   . . . is not impulsive or impetuous and thinks things through carefully

   . . . is very true to his or her own value system

   . . . has neat and orderly work habits

   . . . favors contingency systems to minimize risk

   . . . appreciates the value of quality

   . . . values security and safety

Words that can describe this individual include:

accurate	quiet	clever
analytical	careful	detail-oriented
persistent	precise	perfectionist
skeptical	pragmatic	calm
orderly	thorough	fault-finding

PREDICTABLE

low	high
1	
2	
3	
4	

This individual . . .

    . . . can be seen by others as inflexible

    . . . likes to perform habits, routines, and methods of operating

    . . . is slow to anger, but possesses a strong temper

    . . . prefers a cordial work environment

    . . . works best with structure and rules

    . . . takes pride in his or her performance

    . . . can be a loner and hard to communicate with

    . . . prefers the status quo to change

    . . . is typically a good listener

    . . . has strong powers of focus and concentration

    . . . is a practical thinker

    . . . is usually mild-mannered and controlled

    . . . can be indecisive and vacillating

Words that can describe this individual include:

logical	neat	deliberate
composed	calm	shy
relaxed	consistent	pragmatic
practical	mild	tenacious
reserved	cooperative	loner

EXACTING AND DEMANDING

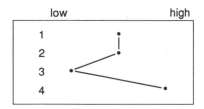

This individual . . .

. . . tends to work calmly with familiar tasks

. . . easily grows bored with routine and repetition

. . . tends to analyze situations before acting

. . . is somewhat resistant to change

. . . places a high premium on detail

. . . tries to avoid risk and threat

. . . can be easily annoyed and can be a complainer

. . . makes decisions based on experience and precedent

. . . is good at reproducing the work of others

. . . seeks to avoid confrontation and friction

. . . wants documentation, structure, and "the book"

. . . is very orderly and organized

. . . shows temper and emotion when threatened

. . . can be highly defensive

. . . tends to be tense, fussy, and worried about accuracy

Words that can describe this individual include:

tense	restless	nit-picking
defensive	orderly	data-oriented
compliant	skeptical	accurate
cautious	worried	self-critical

METHODICAL

This individual . . .

> . . . prefers to carefully examine problems
>
> . . . can be inflexible and resist change
>
> . . . is self-assured and knows "what is right"
>
> . . . can be unpleasant and insensitive if change is demanded
>
> . . . has a strong sense of appropriate behavior
>
> . . . has high personal standards and expects the same of others
>
> . . . can be seen as aloof and uncaring
>
> . . . operates best in a reactive, not proactive, style
>
> . . . can seem unknowable to others
>
> . . . is most productive in a comfortable, stable setting
>
> . . . does not like to initiate action
>
> . . . is the proverbial "iron fist in a velvet glove"
>
> . . . seldom provokes anger, but does possess a strong temper
>
> . . . takes pride in maintaining control and composure
>
> . . . tends to develop strong ties and loyalties

Words that can describe this individual include:

calm	serious	serene
proper	introspective	considerate
satisfied	stable	service-oriented
confident	conservative	deliberate

SOCIALLY ASSERTIVE

This individual . . .

> . . . tends to act quickly in social settings
>
> . . . wants to be involved with people as an end in itself
>
> . . . is highly persuasive and can help to motivate others
>
> . . . feels that goals should be achieved with and through others
>
> . . . can be readily influenced by others who are verbal and poised
>
> . . . enjoys the limelight and public acclaim
>
> . . . is self-assured and self-confident in most situations
>
> . . . can procrastinate and make last-minute decisions
>
> . . . can appear indecisive and vacillating
>
> . . . can be seen as manipulative and insincere
>
> . . . is usually a good delegator
>
> . . . is generally pleasant, outgoing, and positive
>
> . . . stimulates others through enthusiasm

Words that can describe this individual include:

influential	friendly	verbal
outgoing	restless	vacillating
energetic	lively	goal-oriented
poised	confident	socially initiating

CONVINCER

This individual . . .

  . . . prefers to reach goals with and through others

  . . . is generally highly verbal

  . . . uses personal charm to help persuade others

  . . . wants to be liked and looked upon with favor

  . . . sees communication skills as paramount

  . . . has a high need for recognition

  . . . strongly pursues and needs positive relations with others

  . . . is often highly concerned with personal appearance

  . . . is energetic and poised in dealing with people

  . . . usually is opinionated

  . . . is generally seen by others as pleasant

  . . . can be overbearing in pressure situations

  . . . can at times be seen as manipulative and shallow

Words that can describe this individual include:

suave	courteous	charming
extroverted	expressive	goal-oriented
optimistic	cultured	spirited
lively	idealistic	self-assured

CREATIVE

This individual . . .

. . . tends to be highly self-critical

. . . tends to vacillate before making decisions

. . . can be defensive and easily hurt

. . . is action-oriented *after* the facts are analyzed

. . . welcomes change and diversity

. . . works best with a clear reward system administered fairly

. . . may have difficulty delegating

. . . tends to change his or her mind

. . . can think abstractly and be innovative and creative

. . . "works through" issues several different ways

. . . makes decisions independently; is self-sufficient

. . . can be seen by others as a know-it-all

Words that can describe this individual include:

innovative	logical	introspective
pragmatic	creative	precise
exact	conscientious	results-oriented
tense	indecisive	critical
outspoken	methodical	egocentric

ANALYTICAL

```
        low                    high
  ┌─────────────────────────────────┐
  │  1                          •    │
  │  2    •<                         │
  │  3            •                  │
  │  4            •                  │
  └─────────────────────────────────┘
```

This individual . . .

   . . . takes on challenges with prudent risks

   . . . needs an absence of tight controls to work best

   . . . prefers to work alone

   . . . tends to have very high standards

   . . . is generally controlled and unflappable

   . . . has a "show me" attitude and is hard to influence

   . . . requires facts and proof, not assumptions

   . . . takes pride in logical, "tight" conclusions

   . . . tends to be highly independent

   . . . can be direct and even tactless with others

   . . . is a leader when goals are clear

Words that can describe this individual include:

analytical	skeptical	problem-solving
critical	reclusive	firm
cautious	curious	independent
apprehensive	suspicious	competitive

TENACIOUS

This individual . . .

> . . . tends to resist change that he or she did not originate

> . . . usually does not readily join social situations

> . . . works best with systems, precedents, and procedures

> . . . works in a methodical manner; sensitive to deadlines

> . . . enjoys reflective time and solitary time

> . . . can be hard to approach and hard to understand

> . . . is highly composed and does not show emotion easily

> . . . can be highly critical of others' work

> . . . can hold a grudge if others constantly annoy him or her

> . . . is proud of his or her poise and control

> . . . is generally not highly verbal by choice

> . . . prefers projects that can be clearly completed

Words that can describe this individual include:

calm	methodical	socially shy
poised	stable	controlled
cautious	quiet	initiating
loner	rigid	results-oriented
critical	fussy	fault-finder

EXPEDITER

```
        low                    high
    ┌─────────────────────────────┐
    │  1                      •    │
    │  2                  •        │
    │  3           •               │
    │  4                •          │
    └─────────────────────────────┘
```

This individual . . .

> . . . has a very strong drive to achieve results and reach goals

> . . . is self-directed in initiating actions

> . . . prefers change and variety

> . . . makes rapid, firm decisions

> . . . works well with deadlines and pressure

> . . . works best with short-term projects

> . . . searches out better ways to meet objectives; is innovative

> . . . loses patience in uncomfortable situations

> . . . can be insensitive to others, especially when pressured

> . . . can be seen as a "raging bull"

> . . . actively seeks out and uses power

> . . . is a very strong competitor, against others and/or goals

Words that can describe this individual include:

firm	restless	results-oriented
insensitive	tense	direct
initiating	competitive	rises to challenges
innovative	impatient	opportunity-driven

DECISION MAKER

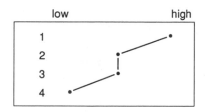

This individual . . .

- . . . requires power and control
- . . . requires responsibility and authority
- . . . readily expresses bold and independent views
- . . . is extremely determined and focused
- . . . generally is dominating and authoritative
- . . . concentrates on getting things done at almost any cost
- . . . is the proverbial "mover and shaker"
- . . . makes independent decisions firmly and quickly
- . . . enjoys challenge, change, and competition
- . . . is a risk-taker
- . . . is a firm and consistent problem solver
- . . . has a need for achievement and self-realization
- . . . can be inflexible in his or her ideas and views
- . . . tends to be an entrepreneur and innovator

Words that can describe this individual include:

progressive	dominating	goal-oriented
independent	firm	self-controlled
inflexible	fair	determined
innovative	assertive	outspoken
competent	confident	powerful

PRACTICAL AND REALISTIC

This individual . . .

. . . welcomes variety and change

. . . enjoys new challenges and is bored by repetition and routine

. . . moves sharply and assertively toward goals

. . . gravitates toward a leadership role

. . . can be seen as a "mover and shaker"

. . . can be seen as self-centered

. . . tends to create new opportunities and challenges

. . . has a need to get things done in the short term

. . . works comfortably with pressure and deadlines

. . . is generally highly emotional and demonstrative

. . . is excellent at start-up and new ventures

. . . can be weak at follow-through and detail

. . . is a risk-taking, quick decision maker

. . . can threaten those who are less self-assured

Words that can describe this individual include:

direct	blunt	decisive
optimistic	enthusiastic	self-assured
persuasive	forceful	firm
outgoing	dominating	self-assertive
focused	restless	high-powered

These profiles can help us understand why we love or hate certain aspects of our job, why we embrace or reject the advice of others, why we are motivated or discouraged by our superiors, and why we forge a team or create divisiveness among our subordinates. In understanding ourselves, we can begin to understand our relationships with others. We can see clues to the motives for others' behavior and, most importantly, can focus on the *causes* of their behavior, rather than on assigning *blame* for their actions.

The closer our behavioral fit with job requirements, the fewer conscious adjustments are necessary for success—on the part of the manager, the employee, or the organization. The poorer the fit, the more conscious, proactive, and constructive are the actions necessary to achieve success, both personal and organizational. These are very basic starting points, no less so than whether a bank teller can count or a pilot can see. Yet while we have math tests and eye exams, we don't usually have behavioral measurements to employ (and wouldn't know what to do with them if we did).

These profiles are intended to form the basis of key managerial measurements and action in an area—behavioral compatibility—that is often overlooked.

Can-Do and Want-to-Do

Do you understand what's required by your job? This isn't as easy a question as it might seem. Job descriptions are notoriously poor for this purpose (when they even exist) because they tend to describe output, activity, and responsibilities. However, of more immediate concern in assessing *compatibility* are input, results, and accountabilities. These are the parameters that can help us determine behavioral fit because they are about "want-to-do," not just "can-do."

One of my career counseling clients epitomized the ability-versus-compatibility problem. She was a straight-commission placement counselor for one of the big personnel franchise chains. Although a top performer, she was unhappy on the job.

"I interviewed well for the job," she pointed out, "and, having scrutinized my resume, the franchise owner told me that I was the most impressive candidate he had ever interviewed. And sure enough, my first year on the job, I was the second highest revenue generator in the office. This year I'll be number one."

Despite her performance, she was experiencing interpersonal problems with the staff, felt her energy level flagging, and found herself indecisive about issues she formerly handled with ease. The problem is one I've observed with many highly talented people—they fail to distinguish between what they *can* do well and what they *want* to do. A person who has a variety of skills, a strong intellect, and a positive self-image can perform in a vast array of jobs. However, whether that person can *sustain* the required performance is quite a different matter.

You've all seen people like this (perhaps in the mirror). They are superb in interviews, and if a living were to be made as a professional interviewee, they would be world-class. They can muster their resources, their wits, and their energies to accomplish almost anything they put their minds to, even without a basic affinity to ease the way. However, after the initial challenge of proving they can do the task, their energy and motivation to sustain the behavior dissipates.

This is precisely what happened to the placement counselor. She placed an extremely high premium on relationships and interaction, and she had very clear values about how people should treat each other. Yet she found herself in a job that, although ostensibly designed to help employer and employee, was in fact part of a "factory" intended to place as many people as possible within a short time. A failure rate—poor matches—was built into the expectations for her job.

This caused tremendous conflict for her. She was torn between her experience as an excellent interviewee and productive recruiter on the one hand, and her innate need to treat people with sensitivity and consideration on the other. Her stress level gradually rose—even while she was performing well—and the resultant frustration began to erode her relationships, her personal life, and her health. Ultimately, her job performance suffered. She was the classic case of someone who can perform a wide variety of jobs, but who can sustain the required behavior for only a few of them. It's imperative that such people have some means of identifying both their native behavioral predispositions and those behaviors required for long-term success in positions they are considering.

Most of us face similar choices. Just because you can do something doesn't mean that you'll like doing it, or will want to continue doing it. One of the best ways of determining this is through a comparison of the behaviors the job requires and those that are native to you. The less stretch required (the less energy invested to change), the more probable it is that you will readily sustain the required behaviors over the long term.

Taking Inventory: Understanding the Job

Here is a brief "job inventory" that includes descriptions of twenty-five job requirements. Simply check yes or no to answer whether your primary job does or does not have each requirement in *most* circumstances. None of the responses is good or bad, so don't try to outsmart the inventory. Just be as honest as you can.

Job Inventory

This job requires in most circumstances:	Yes	No
1. Careful attention to detail	____	____
2. A high degree of accuracy	____	____
3. A minimum of creativity	____	____
4. Close compliance with policy and procedure	____	____
5. More of a detail orientation than a "big picture" view	____	____
6. Repeatedly doing the same components well	____	____
7. High levels of patience and tolerance	____	____
8. Administration of routine chores	____	____
9. More listening and thinking than acting	____	____
10. "Off-the-shelf" solutions instead of innovations	____	____
11. Substantial actions initiated with others	____	____
12. Formal or informal leadership	____	____
13. Application of influence and persuasion	____	____
14. Public appearances and presentations	____	____
15. Relationship-building and consensus-building	____	____
16. Quick, forceful action	____	____
17. Substantial risk-taking	____	____
18. Expediting and problem-solving	____	____
19. Removing or circumventing obstacles	____	____
20. Strong control and firmness	____	____
21. Sensitive, insightful consideration for others	____	____
22. Substantial trust, reliability, and loyalty	____	____
23. Strong self-confidence and self-esteem	____	____
24. High degrees of poise and self-possession	____	____
25. A firm belief in "what's right for me"	____	____

On the scoring key below, record the number of yes responses for each set of job requirements by placing a dot on the appropriate number:

Requirements 16-20	0	1	2	3	4	5
Requirements 11-15	0	1	2	3	4	5
Requirements 6-10	0	1	2	3	4	5
Requirements 1-5	0	1	2	3	4	5
Requirements 21-25	0	1	2	3	4	5

Finally, connect the first four dots to form a pattern. Compare this job inventory pattern to the personal behavior profile you generated earlier. How do they compare? Are they similar?

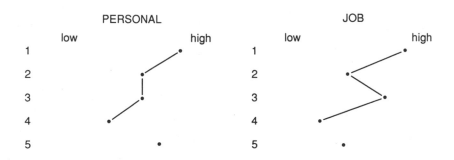

Are they unrelated?

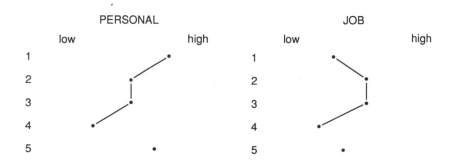

Are they opposite?

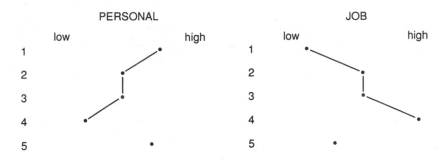

This should be an early indicator of how matched your natural behaviors are to those behaviors required by your job. This match or mismatch has a bearing on your performance, stress, interpersonal skills, and many other workplace demands. We'll examine this relationship in detail in later chapters; here, we'll explore our self-perceptions compared to our actual environment.

Self-Perception and Reality

If perception is so vital in our behavior and performance, self-perception is predominant. If we define the greater reality as that which most people perceive, then there are three possibilities for self-perception:

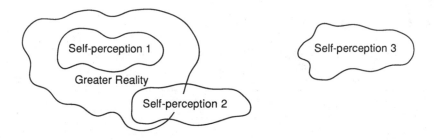

The individual with self-perception 1 is firmly grounded in the greater reality. That means that his or her actions are in accordance with most people's expectations of appropriate behavior. This individual may be dynamic or shy, bold or retiring, but his or her behavior is within accepted mores and norms.

Self-perception 2 belongs to the individual who is astride that reality. He or she may occasionally (or frequently) engage in unorthodox (according to accepted norms) or remarkable behavior. These people may be quite creative: artists, writers, charismatic leaders, and so on. Their behaviors may be seen as quirky, as "flights of fancy," or as simply, "Well, that's Harry!" It has been reported that Confederate General Jubal Early had occasional moments when he thought he was a bird and would seem to peck at imaginary seeds on his collar. Perhaps his subordinates merely said, "Well, that's Jubal," because he was one of Lee's finest generals.

We've all encountered the third type of person. It's the woman who enters a room to be greeted with murmurs of, "How can she dress like that?" Or the manager who concludes a meeting only to have his employees complain, "How can he treat us this way? Doesn't he know what he's doing to morale?" As a matter of fact, the woman thinks she's dressing just fine, thank you, and the manager is quite certain that his actions are the best for the situation. Few people deliberately dress to be gawked at or interact with others to be complained about. However, in such cases self-perception is far removed from the greater reality of shared perceptions and expectations. This is aberrant behavior, based on a set of perceptions far out of the mainstream. Yet what do we usually hear about such behavior? "What do you expect from a woman?" or, "What can you expect from someone with his background?" or, "We shouldn't be surprised with that behavior from someone his age." All these reactions are emotional, prejudicial garbage that clouds our thinking and damages our relationships. Yet such easy ways out are engaged in because they relieve us from the harder work: trying to understand why we act the way we do.

In his classic work, *Self Consistency,* Prescott Lecky notes that:

> We think of ourselves also as belonging to larger groups . . . . If we accept definitions of ourselves as members of groups, it is just as necessary to maintain these definitions as to maintain definitions of ourselves as isolated individuals. Yet if a person does not accept them, he will not maintain them. The criminal is an obvious example.[1]

Compare the words you used to describe yourself earlier in this chapter to those in the description provided in the behavior profile. If they're very similar, you probably know yourself well and have an accurate perception of how you strike others (self-perception 1). If they're slightly different, you may well have self-perception 2—sometimes seen accurately by others (or yourself) and sometimes not. If few or none of the words match your profile, your self-perception may not be grounded in the reality of how most others see you.

Just how much do we become unwitting victims of our self-perceptions, failing to reach our own potential and selling others short? To what degree are we truly unaware of which of the three self-perceptions above pertain to us and which to others?

It can be hard to align our self-perceptions with reality. The primary cause of poor alignment is a lack of feedback. If your car's wheels are out of alignment, you will feel the steering wheel vibrate or experience a pull to the left or right while driving. However, there is no such sensory feedback mechanism automatically alerting us to the drifting of our perceptions. We can all be subject to a "success trap," which is an actual *dulling* of awareness as our successes are routinized.

The Need for Conscious Competency

Try this exercise: To a steady count of one, two, three, four, fold your hands on one and three, and your arms on two and four. So it's hand-arms-hand-arms, through four beats. Ready? Go.

Now, repeat the exercise, but with the *opposite* thumb and arm on top each time you fold your hands and arms. One, two, three, four . . . go.

Notice any difference? If you're like 99.9 percent of your fellow human beings, the second time around was slower and more awkward. We always put the same thumb and arm on top, right or left, for all of our lives. This phenomenon isn't unique to humans. A rattlesnake will always coil in the same direction, clockwise or counterclockwise, for its entire life. These are motor skills, and they become ingrained. (The thumb or arm you place on top is not related to whether you are left-handed or right-handed.)

Behaviors, and even thinking skills, become similarly ingrained to the point where we don't analyze or examine them. For instance, I have difficulty knotting my tie if I think about the individual steps I'm performing. Before you attribute that to my personal shortcomings, think about the people you know who can only do certain things by rote and are lost if they have to start in the middle or explain the component steps. I'm in very good company.

A sequence of competencies can be represented in this manner:

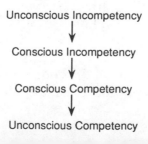

Unconscious Incompetency

↓

Conscious Incompetency

↓

Conscious Competency

↓

Unconscious Competency

When you first folded your hands and arms, you were in unconscious competency. You performed the actions without thinking about them, just as you unconsciously perform aspects of your job and deal with others. When you were asked to put the opposite arm and thumb on top, you were driven back—albeit for a split second—to conscious competency. You had to think about how to do it. The classic example for this sequence starts with the child who can't tie a shoe and doesn't know the shoe should be tied—unconscious incompetency. The child then learns that the shoe should be tied, but can't do it—conscious incompetency. So the child learns how to tie the shoe by concentrating on looping one lace, pulling the other through, and so forth—conscious competency. Finally, the child ties the shoe without thinking about it—unconscious competency.

How much of your job and your relationships are carried on in unconscious competency? This is both the plum and the plague of successful people. While allowing them to perform rapidly and effectively, unconscious competency precludes scrutiny. The only way to evaluate, improve, understand, and communicate about our behaviors is through conscious competency. Your grandmother is unconsciously competent at making chicken soup—a little of this and some of that, who knows? While the soup's great, you can't duplicate it yourself, and even my grandmother's soup tended to vary from batch to batch. That unpredictability might be good enough for soup, but it just won't do as the basis for work relationships and performance.

There are only three basic components of competence in performing any job, be it toll collector, bank teller, or airline pilot. The first is that of basic physical ability. Do you have the physical attributes necessary to do the job, or can you compensate for them? The airline pilot must be able to see and hear and work fine controls. The bank teller must be able to make change and count bills. The toll collector must reach out to cars and collect toll tickets. Physical abilities can be developed—if you need to move heavy boxes you can build up muscles—or compensated for—if you need to move around an office but can't walk, a wheelchair will take care of it.

The second component is skills and knowledge. These are acquired and are usually learnable to varying degrees. The teller must be able to count and fill out certain bank forms. He or she will undoubtedly already be able to count, but may have to undergo training to learn how to complete the forms. The toll collector must be able to give directions, know what to do about toll evaders, spot counterfeit bills, and so on. The airline pilot needs to be able to navigate, understand emergency procedures, and calculate fuel consumption. No one is born with all of the skills for any of these jobs, and no one would naturally acquire them. But all can be learned by some people.

Job Compatibility: Matching Behavior to the Job

Organizations do a fairly good job in testing and evaluating for physical ability and for skills and knowledge. But they virtually ignore the third, equally vital, component: compatible and supportive behaviors. The proper matching of individual behaviors to those demanded by a job is a fundamental element of successful performance, and it is seldom done well. But doing so is especially crucial because there is less opportunity to compensate in this area than in the other two. For example, some jobs require high levels of patience and attention to detail—accounting, underwriting, and surgery, to name a few. An individual with little patience and small attention to detail who, for whatever reasons, is cast into such a position will create havoc not only for the organization but for his or her psyche. Numbers, claims, and lives can be adversely affected, irrespective of the physical ability and knowledge this individual may be applying.

For example, our toll taker is in a boring, highly repetitive job. If he or she has a high patience level, then the job will be a better match for this person than it would be for someone who is highly impatient and craves change and diversity. The more such factors fail to mesh, the more likely it is that conflict, poor performance, and stress will arise. (See Chapter 5 for a discussion of stress and its relationship to job compatibility.) Why would someone with a low patience level accept a job requiring a high patience level, you ask? For the very reasons cited at the beginning of this chapter: pressure from peers, finances, aspirations, and family social pressures. We often pursue jobs and careers for all the wrong reasons, ignoring the most important one of all—how well does the job fit our temperament and predispositions? Our behavior can be modified, but not significantly altered. The manager who is miserable because he is managing a unit that is boring him to tears will not be helped through a pay raise. He will then be a slightly wealthier, bored manager. Organizations are as much at fault for allowing an impatient person to become a toll collector as that person is for seeking the job simply because the benefits are good and the job is secure.

Several years ago, CBS asked my firm to look at a "switchboard problem." Switchboard operators were making fundamental errors, keeping people on hold too long, misconnecting calls, and generally performing poorly. Supervision was changed, to no avail. Management determined that it must be a "training problem" and asked us what kind of training would be best.

The switchboard, to our astonishment, was staffed completely by women with college degrees, some with master's degrees. We found that most had sought out these positions because they were the only ones readily available that were even remotely related to a career in broadcasting, which was their real destination. So these ambitious, assertive individuals had no interest in staffing phone lines and spent whatever time they could exerting pressure to be moved elsewhere. The door was ajar, and they wanted to drag the other foot in. When we asked why these particular hires had been made, we received a not surprising piece of "wisdom": It was thought to be a bargain to obtain such well-educated help at such low pay. Some bargain.

So while organizations do pay attention to physical abilities, skills, and knowledge, they seldom bother to investigate behavioral fit. We all paint pictures of ourselves, especially in interviews or when being considered for other positions. Most of us can do many things. The question is, *do we want to?* I could take the toll taker's test and probably do fine. And I'm sure I could present a fine portrait of a toll collector in my interview. But the job would bore me in twenty minutes, and I'd be quite miserable. My example is an easy one—but what about the people, like you, who are called upon many times during their careers to consider a "better" position, one that carries attractive perks, salary, and benefits, *but one that will make you as miserable as I would be collecting tolls?*

We asked earlier about your dentist's real motivation. Dentists have the second highest rate of suicide among all professions rated. (Psychologists are first.) I know of no scientific study that explains this phenomenon, though many blithely assume that it's somehow got to do with the dentist's depression over being associated with pain. Maybe, but I don't think so. Dentists are graduated from medical school with huge debts for their training and equipment needs. Once established, successful dentists are in a profession that enables them to pay off those sizable bills, as well as establish an affluent lifestyle. Therein may lie the rub.

A successful dental practice is—no pun intended—rooted in the community. Unlike most professionals, a dentist is extremely dependent on his or her established clientele. A dental practice is a sedentary one. Add to this the fact that the job is highly repetitive. Despite advances in dental practice and technology, it is basically about dental hygiene and restoration. Now, place someone in that profession who is highly assertive, who loves change and diversity, and who has low attention to detail, and you'll get a very frustrated and unhappy person.

Certainly, this doesn't describe all dentists. But when the description *does* apply, the discrepancy between natural behavior and job behavior—incompatibility—begins to deleteriously affect performance and/or morale. Why would such a person become a dentist to begin with? For all the wrong reasons we've discussed—because his or her parents were dentists, or the money seemed attractive, or friends were going to medical school. It happens all the time. If you crave change and excitement but your job demands repetition and regularity, something will eventually give.

The finest dentists I've visited *love* dentistry. Ask them about a molar and they'll wax eloquent on the history of tooth enamel. I used to think that this was dreadful stuff, but I've come to realize that the more the dentist is into dentistry, the happier he or she probably is and the better their performance will be. I get *very* nervous around doctors who interrupt a consultation or office visit to take a call from their brokers. In jobs that demand routine and a focus on detail, I want people who thrive on routine and sweat the details with pleasure.

Every day, organizations and their managers are hiring the wrong people to be their "dentists," whether they are underwriting supervisors, salespeople, advertising copywriters, or short-order cooks. How do I know this? Well, because I see it on the job, and so do you. You experience the telephone operators who provide surly assistance, the lawyers who don't return your phone calls, the receptionists who lose messages, and the loan officers who forget to apprise you of all your options. Poor physical ability? Nope. Lack of skills and knowledge? No siree, though the organization might be trying to provide them with more and better "training" to improve their performance. It's their lack of behavioral fit with their jobs, pure and simple.

Our behavior in the workplace is neither random nor preordained. Personal behaviors are the result of self-perceptions, which can—and should—be scrutinized through ongoing feedback. Such feedback can only be effective if we are willing to be consciously competent in our actions and about our impact—not lulled by the trap of success.

The relationships between our personal predispositions, our job-required behaviors, and our self-perceptions might look like this:

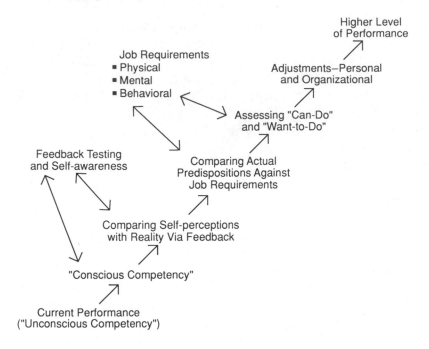

Note that the implications for the manager and the organization are significant—"higher levels of performance." Management practices that focus on behavior issues are essential to effective utilization of human resources. Specifically, management should:

- discriminate between "can-do" and "want-to-do" behaviors in their hiring and selection processes;
- provide feedback mechanisms so that individuals can continually test their perceptions of themselves and others;
- clarify the behavioral requisites for every job;
- ensure that successful performance is constantly and freshly challenged, to avoid the pitfalls of unconscious competency; and
- analyze behavioral fit when evaluating performance and deciding on career tracks.

These are challenging prescriptions, but they are the stuff of peak performance management. The ensuing chapters will provide the understanding and techniques necessary to achieve it.

Note

1. Prescott Lecky, *Self-Consistency: A Theory of Personality* (New York: Island Press, 1951), p. 155.

2

The Mosaic of Behavioral Factors

For free will does not mean one will
but many wills conflicting in one man.
—Flannery O'Connor

Like buying a Ferrari before passing your driver's test, the search for excellence may be somewhat ambitious—or even arrogant—if the fundamentals aren't understood. Your reach should exceed your grasp, we're told. But the object of the reach should at least be within sight.

Many businesses simply don't possess even the basic competencies to survive in the years ahead, much less excel. The competencies are lacking at all levels, from the mail room to the executive suite.

Need proof? Check off the events on this list that have happened to you in the last six months:

____ The phone company gives you a day (it won't give you a time) when it will make an installation or repair. You sacrifice the time and stay home, but the phone people never show up.

____ A credit card company makes an error on your bill that takes phone calls, letters, and months to straighten out.

____ You stand in a bank line that moves like a receding glacier. Several tellers and other bank personnel are happily chatting behind the counter.

____ Your auto repair shop "fixes" something that fails again almost immediately.

____ You can't make a train, plane, or hotel reservation because the reservations lines are constantly busy.

____ You've had trouble—of any kind—with an insurance company.

41

How many have you checked off? Most people check off at least half, and all happen to me regularly. While there are a variety of contributing causes, the common denominator in these situations is a lack of fundamental competence.

In some cases, the absence of competence can be truly sublime. In *The Art of Problem Solving*, Russel Ackoff cites the example of self-imposed constraints creating problems where none exist.[1] In other cases, incompetence can lead to the ridiculous. In order to prove that his landscape business was adversely affected by crossed telephone lines, a friend of mine had to disclose two neighbors' extramarital affairs as part of the evidence that other conversations were intruding on his business line.

Five Behavioral Factors

Being a smart manager tomorrow and the next day requires an understanding of why people act the way they do in various situations, and the ability to predict how they'll act in future situations. This is hard mental work, though well within the capabilities of the average manager. Yet the interest today is in the cheap and quick fixes, formulas that are catchy and slick and enable managers to avoid the hard work. "One-minute management" isn't a quick fix, unless you crave one-minute results. Aphoristic techniques like "management by wandering around" won't accomplish anything if managers don't have the skills, insight, and behaviors necessary to effectively apply such techniques to their own workplaces. Instead, managers need practical approaches that allow them to effectively manage others in any situation, with an emphasis on future success, not past performance.

Here are five basic areas of behavior that represent, singly and in combination, the general spectrum of behaviors we encounter at work. These areas correspond to the five lines of the charts that revealed your behavior profile in Chapter 1:

1. Assertiveness
2. Sociability
3. Consistency
4. Detail Orientation
5. Self-confidence

Remembering that it is the matching of personal behavioral style with job demands that is all-important, let's look at each of these five areas separately. Then we'll look at the whole picture they add up to.

Assertiveness

Collis P. Huntington, founder of the Southern Pacific Railroad, certainly never doubted that the world was his oyster: "Everything that isn't nailed down is mine, and anything I can pry loose isn't nailed down." Assertiveness is the measure of a person's willingness to firmly and forthrightly state a position. Highly assertive people will break into a conversation to express a strongly held opinion, pound a table to make a point, and willingly risk conflict in order to make their positions known (and felt). Unassertive people will tend to refrain from voicing their opinions, especially if conflict might result. They will generally accede to others' opinions, even if it means compromising or sacrificing some personal objectives. Note that these are *general* descriptions: an unassertive person may become highly assertive if a key value or belief is at stake, and a highly assertive person may take a low-key role if, for example, the issue is perceived as minor, or political considerations make it prudent to back off.

The scale below and the other four in this chapter cover the normal range of human behavior. We are not concerned with deviant or aberrant behaviors here, except as they define the outer limits of our scales. For example, extremely high assertiveness can be deemed belligerent, abrasive, or even hostile; extremely low assertiveness can be termed apathetic or unresponsive. We are dealing the normal range of behavior in between these two extremes. (For the scientists among you, on a bell curve we are looking at all responses within one standard deviation.) Our assertiveness scale is thus labeled:

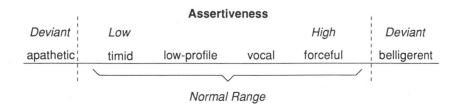

		Assertiveness			
Deviant	*Low*			*High*	*Deviant*
apathetic	timid	low-profile	vocal	forceful	belligerent

Normal Range

Go back to your first set of test results from Chapter 1. Where did you fall on the first line, which measured assertiveness? Remember, this represents where you would be on *most* occasions, not necessarily on all occasions. Here is the chart you used in Chapter 1, aligned with the assertiveness scale.

Assertiveness

	Deviant Low																												Deviant H
①	⋮		⋮	0 1 2		3 4 5 6 7 8		9 10 11 12 13 14 15		16 17 18		⋮
2	⋮		⋮	0 1 2 3	⋮	4 5 6 7 8 9 10 11 12	⋮	13 14 15 16 17 18				⋮
3	⋮	0	1 2 3	4 5	6 7	8 9 10	11 12	13 14	15 16 17	18	⋮
4	⋮		⋮	0 1	⋮ 2 3	4 5	6 7 8	⋮ 9 10	11 12 13	14 15	⋮ 16 17
5	0 1	2 3	4 5	6 7	⋮ 8	9 10	⋮ 11 12	13 14	15	⋮	⋮

Sociability

Sociability is the degree to which a person initiates interpersonal, or social, contact. Highly sociable people make friends and acquaintances easily, readily putting even strangers at ease. They are the "life of the party" and tend to be verbal, animated, and expressive. They seek out and enjoy relationships. "Low-sociability" people prefer *being* approached over doing the approaching. They tend to be more task-oriented than relationship-oriented and can be somewhat uncomfortable when forced to initiate social and/or business contacts. Highly sociable people stride into a business conference of strangers and introduce themselves, immediately beginning to build rapport. The low-sociable slide over to the wall and take in the scene, picking and choosing their spots, hoping someone will seek them out first. (Can you begin to see the value of combining effective behaviors with specific job demands? It's early in the discussion, of course, but who would tend to make the best cold-sell salesperson, and who would tend to be best at working with secret and classified materials?)

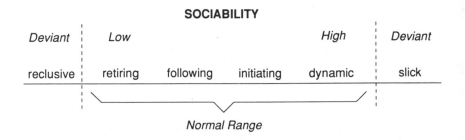

SOCIABILITY

Deviant	Low			High	Deviant
reclusive	retiring	following	initiating	dynamic	slick

Normal Range

Deviantly high sociability is usually seen as "oily" and insincere behavior. "Glad-handers" and politicians, in the most perjorative sense, are those we see as overly sociable. On the low end are hermits and recluses—not just on mountaintops but at work as well. Where did you score on this scale?

Sociability

Deviant Low								Deviant High
1	⋮	⋮ 0 1 2	3 4 5 6 7 8	9 10 11 12 13 14 15	16 17 18	⋮
②	⋮	⋮ 0 1 2 3	⋮ 4 5 6 7 8 9 10 11 12	⋮ 13 14 15 16 17 18		⋮
3	⋮ 0	1 2 3	4 5	6 7	8 9 10	11 12	13 14	15 16 17	18	⋮
4	⋮	⋮	0 1 ⋮ 2 3	4 5	6 7 8 ⋮ 9 10	11 12 13	14 15 ⋮ 16 17 18
5	0 1	2 3	4 5	6 7 ⋮ 8	9 10 ⋮ 11 12	13 14	15	⋮	⋮

You now have two pieces of feedback: assertiveness and sociability. If you scored high on both, you should tend to be forceful, gregarious, extroverted, and equally task- and people-oriented. If you scored low on both, you should tend to be reactive, low-key, wary of risk, and cautious. If you scored high on assertiveness but low on sociability, you should tend to be goal-oriented and task-efficient, and you may prefer to act as an individual contributor. If you scored high on sociability but low on assertiveness, you should tend to be people-oriented and expressive and will prefer to work with and through others in most activities.

Consistency

Those who score high on the consistency scale prefer the status quo. They generally dislike change—especially abrupt change—and enjoy routine and regularity. They may take satisfaction in doing similar tasks over and over, each time achieving consistent and excellent results. People who score low on the consistency scale prefer change, diversity, and variety. They don't feel challenged unless constantly faced with new issues and situations. The lower that people score on this scale, the more nervous energy they possess. Low-consistency people tend to abhor meetings and similar captive events and will often show their impatience through nail-tappping, foot-wagging, and other nervous habits. Deviantly high-consistency people, on the other hand, are in a rut and never want to move out.

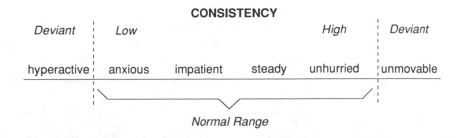

CONSISTENCY

Deviant	*Low*			*High*	*Deviant*
hyperactive	anxious	impatient	steady	unhurried	unmovable

Normal Range

Here is the chart you used in Chapter 1. The mark you placed on line 3 is your consistency score.

Consistency

Deviant Low   Deviant Hig

1	┊		┊ 0 1 2		3 4 5 6 7 8		9 10 11 12 13 14 15		16 17 18		┊
2	┊		┊ 0 1 2 3 ┊ 4 5 6 7 8 9 10 11 12 ┊ 13 14 15 16 17 18								┊
③	┊ 0	1 2 3	4 5	6 7	8 9 10	11 12	13 14	15 16 17	18		┊
4	┊	┊	0 1 ┊ 2 3	4 5	6 7 8 ┊ 9 10	11 12 13	14 15 ┊ 16 17
5	0 1	2 3	4 5	6 7 ┊ 8	9 10 ┊ 11 12	13 14	15	┊		┊

Combining this feedback with prior results, we can observe, for example, that a highly consistent, sociable person will tend to be approachable and nonthreatening and will probably take whatever time is necessary to give others assurances. But that same high sociability combined with low consistency will result in behavior that is more high-pressure, intolerant, and, consequently, more threatening to others. That behavior isn't good or bad, but it does require that both parties understand its source, its impact, and its results.

Detail Orientation

Our last factor is attention to detail. High-scoring people on this scale place a premium on detail, thoroughness, accuracy, and the approval of others. They seek to please and to follow rules, precedent, procedure, and policy. "Low-detail" people tend to be highly independent. They pay little attention to detail and are often more entrepreneurial and precedent-breaking.

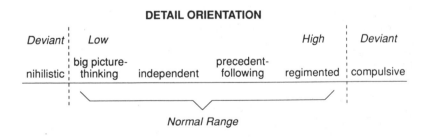

DETAIL ORIENTATION

Deviant	Low		High	Deviant
nihilistic	big picture-thinking	independent	precedent-following	regimented	compulsive

Normal Range

Deviantly low-detail behavior is nihilistic and iconoclastic; deviantly high-detail behavior is submissive and obsessive.

Detail Orientation

Deviant Low																				Deviant High
1		0 1 2	3 4 5 6 7 8	9 10 11 12 13 14 15	16 17 18	
2		0 1 2 3	4 5 6 7 8 9 10 11 12	13 14 15 16 17 18	
3	0	1 2 3	4 5	6 7	8 9 10	11 12	13 14	15 16 17	18	
④		0 1	2 3	4 5	6 7 8	9 10	11 12 13	14 15	16 17 18	
5	0 1	2 3	4 5	6 7	8	9 10	11 12	13 14	15		

With this fourth piece of feedback you should be able to see certain patterns emerge. Behavior that combines high assertiveness with high detail focus will result in demands that even minor details be scrupulously attended to and that problems be segmented, analyzed, and rapidly solved. Low assertiveness combined with high detail orientation characterizes an analytic approach: this person carefully examines details and, if also highly consistent will take a painstaking, slow, and methodical approach to resolving any issue.

It is these combinations on which the descriptions in Chapter 1 of eighteen behavior patterns are based. There are a finite number of combinations of these behavioral traits, and the eighteen patterns reflect those fundamental combinations, not any magic formula. With the examples above, you should be able to develop your own personal feedback. Remember, this testing is not being scientifically conducted, and it is only meant to suggest how you behave *most* of the time. Any of us is capable of change, and we'll examine our change options a little later in this book. But first, we have to look at the final factors.

Self-confidence

The last scale is an approximate measure of self-confidence, social maturity, consideration for others, and, in general, self-esteem.

If you scored high on self-confidence, it means you probably have a very good idea of who you are. Your value system is clear, and you can probably articulate it easily, if asked. You tend to be considerate of others, even in pressure situations, and have a sense of social or business propriety. Moreover, you know what's right for you. Your experience and background have provided you with a "rudder" that tends to keep you steady even in changing winds and tides. When confronted with a setback or unfavorable situation, this sense of self will keep you from becoming overly discouraged. You have perspective on how you might have been at fault, if and how the situation could have been prevented, and what to take from the experience for future use.

SELF-CONFIDENCE

Deviant	*Low*			*High*	*Deviant*
erratic and afraid	unsure of self	situationally comfortable	self-reliant	strongly self-confident	overly rigid and blindly confident

Normal Range

If you scored low, your self-confidence (and perhaps your value system) either isn't fully developed or is in the throes of change, for whatever reason. You may tend to look out for yourself at all costs, considering others only when there is the relative luxury of doing so after your objectives have been met. Your approach to business relationships—and perhaps to social relationships— may be more situational, with your response depending strongly on the specific conditions and personalities involved. People who score low on self-confidence are sometimes new to the business world, young, recently out of school, in a radically new situation, examining their basic beliefs and approaches, and/or not quite certain about their abilities and prospects. As with the other four factors, self-confidence will influence the behavior of the individual in most circumstances.

Self-confidence

Deviant Low   *Deviant Hig*

1		0 1 2	3 4 5 6 7 8	9 10 11 12 13 14 15	16 17 18
2		0 1 2 3	4 5 6 7 8 9 10 11 12	13 14 15 16 17 18	
3	0	1 2 3	4 5 6 7	8 9 10 11 12 13 14	15 16 17 18	
4		0 1 2 3	4 5 6 7 8	9 10 11 12 13	14 15 16 17	
⑤	0 1 2 3	4 5 6 7 8	9 10 11 12 13 14 15		

As with the other factors, the range we've provided covers normal behavior. People off the scale to the right would be excessively self-reliant and would tend to be arrogant, smug, condescending, and rigid. They would be so absolutely convinced of what is right and wrong that they would be doctrinaire and dogmatic. (Philosopher Blaise Pascal once said that evil is seldom done so thoroughly or so well as when it is done with a good conscience.) People off the scale to the left, on the other hand, would be highly unpredictable, operating with situational ethics and guided by short-term interests and needs. They would tend to be unreliable, unsure of themselves, and unsure of relationships with others. In business settings, they would probably place personal interests and well-being ahead of those of their colleagues and the organization.

Here are profiles of two people with different scores on self-confidence. How might these two individuals differ in their behavior when confronted with a highly pressurized situation?

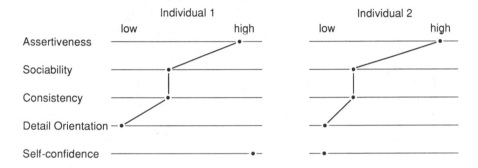

Individual 1 would tend to be cordial, diplomatic, and understanding in relationships with others. Although not excessively sociable, he or she would, nonetheless, be considerate and accommodating. Despite the exigencies of the pressure situation, and despite the tendency to act alone, others *would* be considered. By contrast, individual 2 would tend to be more of a "steamroller" in his or her actions toward others. As the pressure mounted, this person's lack of a strong sense of self-confidence might lead him or her into believing in "letting the chips fall where they may"; as long as the task was completed, this individual might not consider the feelings and treatment of others. Two people with identical profiles would thus act quite differently in the same situation, given the relative strength or weakness of their self-confidence "rudder."

Self-confidence can move in either direction as individuals grow, mature, experience more of life, and learn more about themselves, their capabilities, and the results they have generated in a variety of life situations. This factor, and its position and movement, is often a reliable indicator of whether you are growing, how well you are assimilating lessons, and to what degree you are likely to be able to deal with changing and challenging situations.

Managing Your Energy Battery

All of us possess a "battery." This battery is a physiological fact of life, no less so than the color of our eyes or the span of our reach. Normally, we speak of "bursts of energy," or "flagging energy," and the truth is, we can produce extra energy when needed, conserve our energy, or squander it. Nevertheless, we all have a core energy level that is the basis of our ability to cope with whatever happens.[2]

Some of us have a larger battery than others. But a large battery isn't by definition good, nor a small battery bad. What matters is *how you manage your battery.* Here's a quick test. Who has a larger battery, Ronald Reagan or Jimmy Carter?

When Jimmy Carter was in office, he stayed up to all hours absorbing the details of documents and protocols. He had an insatiable appetite for facts and figures (he is a nuclear engineer by training) and worked long and hard to digest all details. He delegated relatively little—it is alleged that he even determined the scheduling for the White House tennis court. Carter has an enormous battery, capable of sustaining long hours of hard and complex work.

Ronald Reagan made it a practice to take afternoon naps. He frequently visited his California ranch for vacations. He delegated everything that he could, to the point of being accused of not being conversant with key issues. Ronald Reagan has a fairly small battery—a small energy level.

At the conclusion of his four-year term in 1979, Carter addressed Congress. He looked dreadful. Compared with the smiling candidate of only four years earlier, he looked as though he had aged ten years. During *his* tenure, President Reagan was shot and treated for cancer. Yet, after *eight* years in office, he looked better than ever. Carter has a larger battery, but Reagan manages his much better. And politics aside, virtually anyone would conclude that Reagan had the far more productive and noteworthy presidency.

Thus, it's not the size of the battery that's important—it's how well it's managed. Have you ever been warned not to go to a certain manager for a decision late in the day (or even after lunch)? Or to make sure you approach someone else first thing in the morning? In most cases, these are people whose batteries are wearing down at the end of a day, a project, or an assignment.

There are two possibilities for the battery not fitting the job demands: either the job demands a larger battery than the individual has, or the individual has a larger battery than the job requires. For example, the nursing profession demands a large battery. Nurses work long hours in understaffed conditions. They must react to crises while performing their regular, demanding duties. They must be responsible to doctors, hospital administrators, the public, and patients. The energy expenditure is terrific.

If you place someone in that job who happens to have a small battery, what will you get? Burnout, more than likely. But what are the consequences of burnout in the nurse's environment? Well, doctor's orders might not be as rapidly or as effectively carried out. Patient calls might not be responded to as quickly. Families might not be treated with the courtesy and tact that they are due. Mistakes in medication might occur. Symptoms might be misdiagnosed. In other words, the illness could be made worse. Death could occur. (There is a word for illness caused by the health professional or organization—"iatrogenic.") So burnout is only a euphemism for saying that other people can suffer when a key person's battery is not sufficient for the task at hand.

How many people are suffering from insufficient management batteries? That is, how many people are mismanaged, mishandled, and mistreated because a manager's battery is not large enough for meeting his or her management responsibilities well? Unfortunately, there are many such managers and they are all around us. An insurance underwriting job typically requires a low-energy battery. An underwriter doesn't work with customers, and seldom with colleagues. The job involves applying actuarial and risk procedures found in manuals to the conditions stipulated about the proposed insured in their applications. It is a methodical and routine job and can be performed well by someone with a low energy level.

If you place a large-battery person in the underwriter's job, you'll get boredom. The results will be errors of omission or, perhaps, creative underwriting, which is the last thing the organization needs. Yet this is the inevitable result of putting high-energy performers in low-energy positions.

A serious, contemporary business problem has come to be known as "white-collar moonlighting." The moonlighting manager runs a consulting service or other business "on the side," but in actuality often from his or her own desk during the day. A supervisor at a water processing plan in Cranston, Rhode Island was found to have worked on his job for only about thirty minutes a day for over ten years, spending the rest of his time running assorted business activities from his plant desk. "I could do the job in thirty minutes, and no one ever complained about my work—what harm was done?" the supervisor asked when finally discovered by stunned superiors. Moonlighters are people whose energies are not consumed by their work. Their talents, interests, and abilities seek other outlets. Some of us take up bass guitar in rock bands, others play racquetball, and many moonlight.

There is rarely a perfect match between individual energy level and the energy required by a job, but the two should be fairly close, or adjustments should be made by the individual and the organization to compensate for the differences. To leave serious discrepancies to the fates is the height of irresponsibility.

Ensuing chapters will discuss behavior change and what degree of change is available to us. But you should be able to see already that the larger one's battery, the more one is able to sustain large behavior changes. This is because behavior change isn't simply a matter of choosing to sit on a chair or on a couch. It's more analogous to a right-handed person choosing to begin using the left hand to perform certain tasks (or vice versa). As the tasks become more complex and finer motor skills are required, the more energy and concentration are required to master the change. Eventually, there comes a point where there is insufficient energy and concentration available—and this varies from individual to individual—to make the change. For example, in the activities below, changing from one's natural handedness to the other would require increasing energy and concentration:

Building a Delicate Scale Model   ↑

Throwing a Ball Accurately

Drawing a Simple Picture

Using Scissors

Using a Calculator

Opening a Combination Lock |

Increasing
Energy
Demand

As you proceeded to the more difficult motor skills, increased frustration would be likely to accompany the demand for increased energy.

The same principles apply to behavior change. As the tasks involved in the change become more alien to natural behaviors, more energy and concentration are required to master the change. And the *longer* the change is required, the greater the energy "discharge."

Outlined below are activities in which a low-assertive manager might have to invest increasing energy to meet new behavioral demands:

Full-time Sales Position in Competitive Market
Manage a Unit with a Troublemaking Union
Control Daily, Boisterous Staff Meetings
Regularly Discipline Intransient Subordinates
Complain to Vendors About Poor Service
Control Weekly One-Hour Sales Meetings

Increasing
Energy
Demand

And the behavioral demands of these activities would require that a low-detail person might have to invest increasing amounts of energy:

Be a Full-time Research Analyst
Complete Weekly Corporate Tax Returns
Perform Daily Statistical Analyses
Administer Production Reports
Check Validity of Sales Forecasts
Complete Expense Report

Increasing
Energy
Demand

By the same token, a basically inconsistent person can become much more consistent if he or she has a large battery from which to invest energy into the change. Or an unassertive person can assume a greatly heightened assertive posture if his or her battery can sustain the extra output. But if the battery isn't large enough to sustain the change, the person will run down. The greatest single result of this is stress, and that will be discussed further in Chapter 5.

You should be able to easily see this phenomenon in your own behavior. If you're doing something comfortable—that is, consistent with your basic behavioral predispositions—you can coast along pursuing that activity for long periods. If you're doing something inconsistent with your basic behavioral set, you'll feel fatigue and tension much sooner. For example, I have a low attention to detail, but if I'm asked to perform detail work for a short period, I can do it. Over long periods, however, I become irritable and anxious. If my battery were smaller than it is, I would feel this stress even sooner and more acutely, or I might be incapable of doing detail work at all. Those of you who scored low on detail orientation probably share this experience.

Conversely, I once worked for a boss who paid extremely high attention to detail and had a high patience level. He felt the greatest treat in the world was to spread out his work on the floor and work on it all night. Yet if we pressured him for a quick decision, he became stressed and anxious. He happened to have a small battery. Although the job demand—making an immediate decision—seemed minor to us, the behavioral effort—moving out of his native behavior to meet what we demanded—was immense for him. The greatest battery drains occur when we're forced to change behaviors.

Using the Five Behavioral Factors to Manage Others

As you manage others, you should be assessing current and projected job performance in conjunction with the behaviors required and the behaviors available. Here are some situations that you may (and probably do) encounter on the job. Write down three things you might do to improve the situation. Then compare your responses to the recommended ones that follow.

Scenario 1. Your subordinate is the best customer service person in the company. She is consistently praised by customers for her careful, thoughtful, and patient work on their site. And her work never has to be checked or fixed. She is cordial and cooperative with everyone, but cannot be rushed. In fact, her average number of calls per week is 15 percent less than that of others in similar jobs, and her paperwork is perpetually late because she takes so much time with it.

Her consistency and detail orientation are very high:

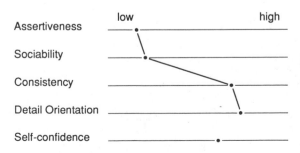

What might you do to increase her call rate and get her paper-work completed on time?

1. _____

2. _____

3. _____

Scenario 2.   Your colleague is very gregarious and outgoing, and also highly inconsistent. You have a hard time working with him on a joint project you've been assigned because he tends to be verbal and dynamic but not very analytic or systematic. He assumes things will get done but, even with the best intentions, has trouble following through to ensure that the details are attended to. You want to not only get the project completed on time but to preserve a constructive working relationship with your colleague, whose profile looks like this:

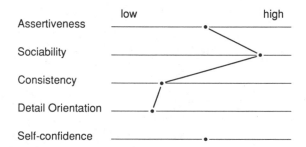

What might you do to make sure that the project makes head-way and that nothing falls between the slats, realizing you can't do it all yourself?

1. _____

2. _____

3. _____

Scenario 3.   Your boss seems to be in a "worry rut." His confidence in himself is low—he's always trying to assess "which way the wind is blowing" and what his superior may be thinking. Not much of a risk-taker, your boss is very unassertive and, while pleasant and outgoing, reacts poorly to change. Yet you have a proposal to restructure your department that requires his approval. The restructuring will provide a tremendous productivity boost for your area of responsibility.

Your boss's profile is:

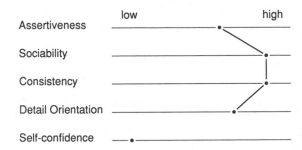

What might you do to get your restructuring approved without delay or procrastination?

1. _____

2. _____

3. _____

Recommended Responses

All of these scenarios are taken from actual incidents. The responses recommended below are based on behaviors, not on bias or emotions or reputations. These aren't the only effective responses, but they should demonstrate what some appropriate actions might be.

Scenario 1.
   1. Provide a "time check" for each phase of the service work, against which she can compare progress.
   2. Provide preprinted paperwork, requiring only check-offs of categories, not written explanations.
   3. Ask her to analyze how routine service calls can be reduced and to then implement her ideas.

These actions appealed to the service representative's detailed, consistent manner. Change was not *demanded* nor did her manager threaten, "Increase your call rate or else!"—an approach that fails to consider behaviors at all. Note also that her manager was able to provide some simple job aids to make her behavior change controllable. Finally, she was able to use her native detail orientation in changing her work behaviors.

Scenario 2.
1. Assign a subordinate to your project team to track and report on details.
2. Create an agenda for every meeting with objectives to be met.
3. Talk once a day by phone between meetings to follow up on progress.

The gregarious colleague reacted well to frequent phone calls and another person on board and welcomed the help with tracking details. In addition, he was forced to adhere to the agenda because it was visible and focused. Note how much more positive these actions based on behaviors are than those based on blame. ("He doesn't want to carry his load—well, I'm not doing more than my share," or, "Everything falls through the slats—he's an incompetent, and I'm letting the boss know why this project will fail.")

Scenario 3.
1. Provide a detailed evaluation of the projected improvements, and show how similar proposals were embraced by your boss's boss.
2. Request that both of you present the idea to your boss's boss, with you making the pitch and taking responsibility if it's poorly received.
3. Arrange for an informal lunch meeting between the three of you during which you mention the idea and allow your boss to hear his superior's candid, but informal reaction.

The idea here is not to further threaten or erode your boss's confidence by forcing him to make a quick decision. You want to make assurances and encourage acceptance, working with your boss in a supportive manner. Circumventing him, threatening him, or ignoring him will not result in long-term improvement and only makes the problem worse since these actions further erode your boss's self-confidence.

These have been just brief examples of using behaviors—as opposed to presumed motives, unnecessary training, or various "inspirational" techniques—to manage and influence others. We'll talk more throughout the book about the role these behavioral factors play in managing people, but for now some relationships should be clear:

- Poor performance is not necessarily a skills, training, or motivation problem. It may well be a behavioral mismatch between the person and the job. But where do most managers almost always immediately invest their time and energy when confronted with poor performance?

- Rarely do job and person form a perfect behavioral match. Usually there are manageable adjustments and accommodations that can be made—both personal and systemic—that can result in the desired performance.

- Behavior change is possible for all of us, but it is determined by the *extent* of the change required, the necessary *duration* of the change, and the *capacity* of one's battery to support that extent and duration.

The Mosaic Assembled: The Job Picture

Here are three common outcomes of comparing personal and job behavioral profiles.

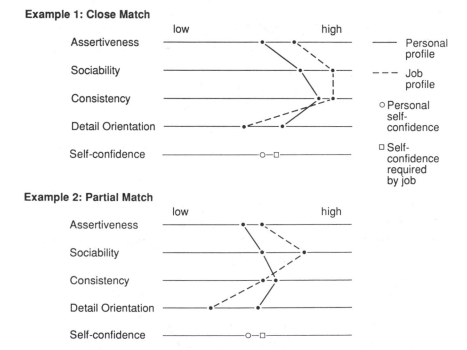

Example 3: Poor Match

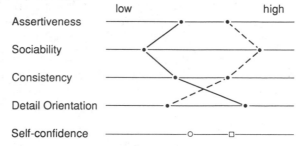

The angles and slopes of the lines highlight the degree of compatibility between personal and job profiles. Generally, if the personal and job lines are in the same relative positions, as they are in example 1, the match is solid. If the two lines deviate somewhat, there is a partial match. In example 2, note that the slopes between sociability and consistency are opposite. In other words, this job scores highest in sociability, but the individual possesses consistency as the predominate behavior, with a far lower degree of sociability.

Use two different colors to record below on the same chart your personal profile from Chapter 1 and your job profile from the inventory later in that chapter.

	low	high	
Assertiveness			
			Personal profile color:
Sociability			Job profile color:
Consistency			
Detail Orientation			
Self-confidence			

The closer your lines above come to example 1, the more identical your personal and job profiles will be; the more they resemble example 3, the more dissimilar they will be.

You may wish to perform the same exercise for jobs and people for whom your are responsible. Have you placed people in positions for which their behaviors make sense? If not, have you provided job aids—personal or systemic—to help reconcile the differences between job behavioral demands and natural predispositions? Have you investigated behavioral incompatibility when you've encountered performance problems, or have you always assumed that you're confronting a skills, knowledge, or motivational problem?

And what about career tracks and succession planning? Are you preparing people for future jobs in such a way that behaviors have been understood and considered? Or are you in effect simply saying to them, "Here's the ball, you know how to run, go for it"?

When you seek to influence others, inside or outside of your direct control, do you evaluate their behavioral styles in deciding on the most effective way to approach them? Or do you simply concentrate on "being you," without regard for the impact on them?

We raise these questions because they are the very essence of successful management. They are the difference between vaguely seeing this:

and clearly seeing this:

"HIGH-ASSERTIVE" PERSON IN "LOW-ASSERTIVE" JOB	"LOW-DETAIL" PERSON IN "HIGH-DETAIL" JOB

What do we do with something as vague as a "communications breakdown" (or a "personality conflict," or "poor chemistry")? And how do we know its causes? How can we prevent it to begin with?

The second way of looking at performance problems accounts for behavioral fit, rather than relying on blame, intuition, or biases. We have realized that personal and job profiles are askew, and we have tangible, discrete options at our disposal for dealing with these discrepancies. We can modify the job (systemic change), provide job aids for the performer (performance change), or modify our own expectations (personal change—"I'm reconciled to the fact that Joe's expense reports are always a week late. It's a minor annoyance that I can live with.").

Training people, motivating people, and, generally, trying to ride herd on people will be a frustrating, expensive, and worthless experience if the performance problem is behavioral. You can't train someone to be more sociable; you can't motivate someone to be less attentive to detail; you can't harass someone to be more, or less, consistent.

So step back—perhaps way back—and view the mosaic you create from developing the personal and job profiles and comparing the two. Does the big picture make sense to you in terms of:

- Current performance
- Future performance needs
- Career planning
- Interpersonal relationships
- Management responsibilities
- Work assignments
- Responsibilities

The following chapters will suggest management tools and techniques intended to keep the personal/job mosaic clear and well balanced.

Notes

1. Russell Ackoff, *The Art of Problem Solving: Accompanied by Ackoff's Fables* (New York: John Wiley & Sons, 1978), p. 9.
2. For a discussion of energy as it relates to human endeavors, see John D. Ingalls, *Human Energy: The Critical Factor for Individuals and Organizations* (Reading, MA: Addison-Wesley, 1976).

3

The Limits of Behavior Change

The unexamined life is not worth living.
—Socrates

Carly Simon is a well-known, highly regarded singer who rarely performs in public. Her lack of exposure, however, is neither the strategy of a calculating rock star nor the idiosyncrasy of a moody artist. Carly Simon is scared of appearing in front of a live audience. Before concerts, she vomits and almost loses control of her emotions. And this from someone who produced an album featuring her on the cover dressed in nothing but a brief slip and a provocative glance.

Barbra Streisand shares this fear and had to work diligently to entertain 500 guests at a political fund-raiser she hosted at her own home. We often attribute the actions of an illusive entertainer or a temperamental athlete to disrespect, ingratitude, or poor breeding. In actuality, whether we're trying to understand a John McEnroe, a Sean Penn, or a Don King, other factors may be at work.

Limits: What We All Have in Common

Just because an individual's behaviors are appropriate for success in a particular area doesn't mean they are transferable to other areas. Marshall MacLuhan talked about the "mixed media effect" that prompts us to vest people with expertise in *one* area with expertise in *all* areas.[1] Thus, we listen to an excellent actor discuss politics, allow a politician to write a review of a novel, and create the television "personality"—people who apparently have no other claim to fame except that they *are* television personalities, miraculously created as one is born Italian, or becomes a Republican. Where else could Dick Cavett, Dennis James, and Betsy Palmer have come from?

Similarly, we expect excellent athletes to be able to handle the intrusive media, and we can't understand why Marilyn Monroe seemed so haunted by publicity. Wouldn't anyone love to have such problems? Bring on the press!

But what is there in the ability to hit a ball over a net or sing a haunting ballad that prepares one for dealing with rapid-fire questions, deliberate innuendo, and high-voltage interpersonal communications? How many of us can stand up to that kind of pressure and scrutiny?

Here's another quick self-evaluation. Write below your three greatest fears, whether or not you feel you successfully deal with them. In your occupation and life, what three things create the most tension, angst, and general discomfort for you?

1. _____

2. _____

3. _____

According to *The Book of Lists,* among the general population the top three fears are:

1. Fear of public speaking
2. Fear of heights
3. Fear of insects and bugs[2]

For those of us who make a living at it, it's hard to imagine, but fear of addressing a group of peers is one of the most common fears of most people. If that's the case, why should we be so surprised when a movie actor stammers at a live awards ceremony (this is why the Tony awards for Broadway theater excellence are usually the most polished of the awards shows— the participants are used to performing live), or when an athlete is functionally incoherent in a postgame interview? In fact, there are large firms teaching businesspeople how to deliver presentations and overcome their discomfort. But why should a linebacker subject himself to developing such a peripheral behavior?

Years ago, Willie Mays was a guest of honor on "The Ed Sullivan Show." He emerged from behind a curtain to appear alone, center stage, before a deafeningly loud studio ovation and untold millions behind the camera's lens. Mays was virtually traumatized. It was clear that no one had adequately prepared him for this lonely, frightening moment, and he literally lost control of his actions. There on stage, before millions of adoring fans, the Say-Hey Kid engaged in a personal habit that our mothers have admonished us never to do. He picked his nose. There was nowhere for the camera to discreetly look off. Such can be the results of pressure to behave at great variance with our native predispositions.

Why do some of us comfortably address groups, or put strangers at ease, or deal with complex details, while others go through sheer agony under identical conditions? Why do some managers do better than others in raising morale, managing a crisis, or training a successor? Why can't we simply emulate a good speaker, a patient counselor, or a "life of the party"?

The reason, of course, is that we're talking about *behavior,* not *skills.* Skills can be learned through assimilation and repetition of discrete steps. Behavior, however, can only be modified, and even then only within a certain range and only by subtle and individualized means.

The key to behavior change is *sustaining* the change. Virtually anyone can change behavior briefly—it's changing it and maintaining it over long periods that's the trick. These are the primary factors that will determine one's success in modifying behavioral predispositions:

1. The battery: How much energy is available to invest in the required change?

2. The degree of change: Are we asking a person who hates detail to be scrupulously detailed, or are we asking a moderately detail-oriented person to be slightly more thorough?

3. The duration of the change: Is an unassertive person being asked to firmly run a two-hour meeting once a week, or is that person being placed in an aggressive sales manager's role full-time?

4. Feedback and reinforcement: Is the individual aware of the effects of the changed behavior, and is that behavior related to his or her own self-perception and self-esteem?

As I mentioned in Chapter 2, I'm a fairly low-detail person. When I was young, I began collecting stamps. It was pleasant and educational to mount them in the album. As I matured and my sophistication grew, my collecting became influenced by the increasing sophistication of the hobby and of philatelists. I joined the American Philatelic Association; my collection became specialized by country; I became concerned with watermarks, perforation varieties, plate numbers, glue condition, counterfeits, restorations, color variations, precancels, overprints, and errors. I found myself subscribing to four different stamp periodicals, bidding in six regular mail auctions, and participating in two mail sales circuits. I'd return from business trips realizing that I had to catch up on my stamp work.

Work?

My hobby had engaged so many behaviors that are "work" for me that I had begun to think of it as another job! The detail, minutiae, and excruciating thoroughness ("How to Recognize Perforation Errors Among 19th-Century Revenues" was one memorable article) had ruined my pleasant little hobby. More was *not* better.

If you find that an avocation, an occupation, or even a relationship doesn't seem as rewarding as it once was, remember that conditions *can* change. To be an effective travel agent ten years ago didn't require nearly the attention to detail that is demanded today, with deregulated carriers, labyrinthine routings and prices, and more people traveling than ever before. Fifteen years ago, an effective police officer didn't need the patience of one today, who must remember proper police methods, due process, individual rights, and restraint of unnecessary force. Over that time span, changing conditions have also affected most managers and professionals. In the office workplace, issues such as sexual harassment, substance abuse, unfair termination, affirmative action, and a shrinking labor pool demand vastly different responses from management today than was the norm a decade ago.

Few of us have the luxury of never having to try to modify our behavior—not if we want to continue to grow and excel. And as managers, we must become adept at helping others change as well if we are to achieve results through people.

Techniques to Change Behavior

There are three primary methods usually employed to achieve behavior change: applying coercive power, activating peer pressure, or appealing to rational self-interest.

Coercive Power

This is the "big stick" method whose adherents generally believe that you're likely to get someone's attention by first giving him a few solid whacks to the head. The power approach to behavior change—whether the power is derived from authority, threat, fear, or deprivation—is always short-lived. It's effective only as long as the coercion is being applied. And big stick methods are always vulnerable to someone else's even bigger stick. Power applied in this manner creates *movement*, not motivation.

"Jones, if you don't take a harder line with your customer service reps, you're gonna be looking for other work." That's a typical power threat, from the old-line school of management. If Jones scores low on the assertiveness scale, this threat can have only a few outcomes:

1. Jones can't be more assertive, the boss continues to threaten, and poor customer service performance continues much longer than it needs to.
2. Jones tries to be more assertive, isn't very good at it, and makes his performance even worse while adding to his stress level.
3. Jones opts out of the job, literally or figuratively.

Trying to change behavior through threat and fiat is doomed to fail, largely because the approach assumes that anyone's behavior is readily changeable. This approach ignores each individual's behavioral predispositions and fails to consider the question, "For how long and at what price am I asking this individual to change behaviors?"

Peer Pressure

There is a normal human desire to be "in with the in crowd." Consequently, we are overtly or covertly pushed toward behavior that conforms to that of our colleagues and peers.

The more homogeneous the culture—or the more controlled—the greater the potential impact of peer pressure. On a grand scale, for example, the government of Singapore is able to promote courtesy months, fitness weeks, and clean-up campaigns on a nationwide basis. And, as opposed to similar attempts in less controlled cultures, they work.

Peer pressure–motivated behavior change has its own set of limitations:

1. "In" things change; too often, they're fads and trends. There's no long-lasting assurance that the forces influencing the modified behavior will continue.
2. The modified behavior can cause significant stress for the individual if the "stretch" required is greater than what comes naturally.

3. This type of change seldom influences highly independent, assertive, and/or forceful people. The maverick will actively reject any such attempts to influence his or her behavior.

"Jones, can't you be on the team with the rest of us? We're after participation from the front-line people to achieve our quality goals. So get out there with the rest of us and talk to people—get them involved!" Talk about stressful alternatives—initiate acutely uncomfortable exchanges with those you manage, or let the team down!

So while we see bankers sprouting mustaches en masse, yellow ties suddenly adorning blue suits, or hemlines rising and falling with the tides, such "go with the flow" behavioral changes are best left to lemmings. Peer pressure is also no more than a kind of movement. It doesn't genuinely motivate, and therein lies its fatal flaw.

Rational Self-interest

This approach is based on a very simple premise. If people realize that a given change makes their lives, jobs, and/or relationships better, they will tend to make it and sustain it for as long as the improvement lasts. (Contrast these three change agents—power, peer pressure, self-interest—to how children are taught in school: 1) "Learn your multiplication tables or you'll stay after school"; 2) "Don't you want to be like all of your friends and be able to recite the multiplication tables?" 3) "If you learn the multiplication tables, you'll be able to figure out how many days we have left until summer vacation.") A bank teller who is ordered to tell customers about a new loan product will do so only as long as the head teller keeps track. If the teller is asked to promote the product because all of the tellers are doing so, he or she will do it for as long as the others keep it up. But if the teller is given a reward (money, recognition, time off), he or she will promote the product for as long as the reward is attractive, irrespective of what others do.

	Movement	Motivation
Source	external	internal
Duration	short-lived	long-lived
Stimulators	outside influences	self-perpetuating
Scope	only as far as needed	constantly seeking to expand
Focus	pleasing others	pleasing oneself

True motivation can only be self-induced. I can't *motivate* you in the sense of *moving* you. But I can try to establish an environment in which you are more likely to feel motivated on your own. This is the opposite of "movement."

By appealing to self-interest, we enlist the individual in the act of behavior change. Of the three primary sources of behavior change, only the pursuit of rational self-interest allows permanent change to occur.

True appeals to self-interest will involve external factors (money, status, responsibilities) as well as internal factors (feeling good about oneself, gratification, a sense of well-bing). The efficacy of these appeals varies tremendously, and appeals to internal factors are particularly dependent on the varying degrees of self-esteem from one person to the next.

The Role of Self-Esteem in Changing Behaviors

Virtually all of us suffer from some chinks in our self-esteem. Let's take a brief look at the role of self-esteem in our current and desired behavior patterns.

Self-esteem isn't just thinking well of yourself. It is also a *consistent* feeling of self-respect. Self-esteem shouldn't vary, despite trouble at work, personal setbacks, and "bad days." Self-esteem is strongly related to self-confidence—it is a rudder, a stabilizing influence, a "centering." High self-esteem provides control and a sense of what's right for the individual.

Many everyday concerns can damage our self-esteem, which happens to virtually all of us in one form or another. But self-esteem is improvable and is one of the key elements in effective behavior change.

Three factors influence the strength of your self-esteem:

1. Reinforcement. When you perform well or accomplish some worthwhile task, your manager must provide genuine reinforcement for your success. Everyone knows the difference between hearing, "Great job! Let's make sure we show everyone!" and hearing, "Uh, that's nice. Have you made any progress on the other projects?" The traits that are reinforced by the first comment build into confidence, self-centering, and self-esteem.

A hotel front-desk manager stops to say to a registration clerk: "Nice way you handled that irate guest who felt he had a better rate reserved—he left with a smile on his face. I couldn't have done it better myself." This manager has made a tremendous contribution to perpetuating positive self-esteem, even in the face of harassment and angry customers.

2. Perspective.   Proper perspective is, "Don't worry—this, too, will pass." Poor perspective is, "You've probably ruined your entire career!" Maintaining a healthy perspective alleviates anxieties and stress. Its absence can lead to depression and artificial stimulants. Good perspective holds that rudder steady by creating a sense of where you are in the larger scheme of things.

The manager who counsels a subordinate with, "All right, you made a bad decision in submitting such a complicated proposal, but what does this tell us about the ones we still have to submit?" is creating constructive perspective. The manager who simply warns, "That was strike two," is creating a very different one. Self-esteem relies heavily on the freedom to fail.

3. Mentors.   Effective role models illustrate a sense of discipline and worth through their achievements. Those role models who actively counsel others are often called "mentors."

Mentors build self-esteem by serving as the "objective other" who can provide accurate, unbiased, yet personal feedback to the individual. It's not unusual to find even senior managers seeking out a personal mentor, and many firms have introduced a formal process wherein junior people are taken under a senior person's wing. (In such an "assigned" system, it's important to understand whether the wing belongs to an eagle or a turkey.)

Highly successful overachievers may actually suffer from *low* self-esteem. Constant achieving is an external replacement for internal self-fulfillment. One indicator that self-esteem is low is a feeling of emptiness or self-doubt, despite job success and financial security. Some suggestions for managers:

- Don't exacerbate lows and defeats. Don't be overly hard on others' initial mistakes. Accept people as human, with strengths and weaknesses, and understand that we all experience ups and downs. Remember that self-esteem is a *consistent* good feeling about yourself—and a feeling that you can nurture in others.

- Value play time as much as work time. Don't feel guilty about enjoying yourself, and don't insist that others be workaholics. At times, go with your impulses and hunches about people without feeling the need to analytically justify your actions.

- Evaluate your relationships. Don't develop relationships only with those who have low self-esteem. Serve as a role model exemplifying self-worth and self-fulfillment to others.

- Provide reinforcement for others' successes and victories. Seek out other people who can also perform this role, and make it a daily part of management.

- Understand that self-esteem is internally generated. Don't confuse it with making a certain amount of money or achieving a given business goal. You must be able to be happy with yourself *in spite of* outside influences. And you must encourage others to attain this self-fulfillment.

Self-esteem is as important as energy level and self-interest in the formula for changing one's behavior. Everyone can't do everything, and the degree of possible behavior change is finite. But these elements are the parameters within which we can consciously and intelligently modify our own behavior, as well as that of others. They constitute what we *can* do (energy level), what we *want* to do (rational self-interest), and what we *would* do (self-esteem).

Behavior change is often intellectually accepted at the same time it is being emotionally rejected. "I must change my behavior," and, "I really must stop acting like that," are, as we all know, easier said than done. In our striving for self-consistency, we unconsciously drive for equilibrium—that is, assuming behaviors that are congruent with our self-perceptions.

A Citibank personnel officer in Singapore asked for my help in evaluating a key staff member's behavior. "My colleague paints a mask," she explained. "She sees herself as innocent and personable, yet she is in reality quite threatening and intimidating to those around her." Her colleague, however, was being quite consistent: her self-perception was that of a charming, personable woman, and to *her*, her behavior reflected that demeanor. She was oblivious to her colleagues' differing perceptions because they gave her no feedback to indicate that her behavior was at odds with her image. Peers reacted to her with courtesy, even while dreading contact with her overbearing nature. Their reinforcement was consistent with her behavior.

We were able to modify her assertive behavior by appealing to her self-interest and self-esteem through structured feedback. Using a behavioral profile testing device in which her colleagues anonymously participated, she began to understand the actual effects of her behavior on others—that is, what their shared perceptions were, and how they were covering for her with their artificial civility. She realized that she could expend less effort and get more honest reactions (greatly in her self-interest) if she toned down her approach, listened more carefully, and didn't insist on getting her way in every minor matter.

We all seem to possess an internal gyroscope that keeps our behaviors consistent with our self-image. Reorienting the gyroscope calls for valid feedback—a real demonstration that the current course might not be the best one for realizing our goals. Loren Eiseley has remarked that "some coasts are set aside for shipwreck." Those dangerous coasts encountered on the human journey are those where feedback has been missing and one's behaviors are not productive for a given environment and relationships. Consequently, a primary, ongoing function of management is to provide accurate, constructive feedback for subordinates (and colleagues)—not a once-a-year formal evaluation, but a continuous process of nurturing self-esteem.

Reactions to Change:
Opportunity or Threat?

It is often difficult to emotionally accept change, especially in behavior that we've always deemed consistent with our self-perception. Try this brief exercise: Think of your business colleagues, friends, family, and acquaintances. In the spaces below, list the names of those who react to change as indicated.

Reactions to Change

These people immediately view change as *opportunity.*	These people immediately view change as *threat.*
1. _____	_____
2. _____	_____
3. _____	_____
4. _____	_____
5. _____	_____
6. _____	_____

7. _____   _____

8. _____   _____

9. _____   _____

10. _____   _____

Which list is longer? In most cases, the right-hand side will be longer, or at least much easier to complete. Which list do you appear on?

How can managers present change as opportunity, not threat? By adopting these habits:

- Don't encourage "we win/they lose" competitions.
- Don't begin explanations with, "We've always done it this way."
- Don't ever say, "Yes, *but*..."
- Don't be concerned with blame and culpability.
- Don't accept yes-men as valued subordinates.
- Tolerate failure in a good cause—the freedom to fail.
- Require new solutions to old problems.
- Spend formal meeting time on innovation.
- Try to "leapfrog," not keep up with, the competition.
- Ask "why not" instead of "why."

Take another look at the names you've listed. On which side are the most successful people, irrespective of how you may define "success"? The more successful (or "happy," or "fulfilled," or "motivated") are usually to be found on the left-hand list. That is because they are open—intellectually and emotionally—to the necessity of change. While we tend to vary, individual to individual, in the *degree* to which we can change, our *willingness* to change is a different factor altogether. Consequently, an individual with a small ability to change, but a willingness to do so, will be much more flexible and resilient than a person with a large capacity for change, but no desire to do so.

Reactions to Change

Change as Opportunity	*Change as Threat*
Promising	Dreading
Motivated	Depressed
Courageous	Fearful

Experimenting	Cautious
Innovative	Repetitive
Poised	Awkward
Expansive	Protective
Flexible	Rigid
Confident	Doubtful
Leader	Follower
Daring	Conservative
Extroverted	Introverted
Aware	Unaware
Decisive	Vacillating
Proactive	Reactive

Take another look at your list of people. Do the words on the left above roughly describe those in your left-hand column? Which set of words best descibes you? Your key subordinates? Your immediate boss? Your closest colleagues?

The tendency of people to regard change as implicitly threatening is a core obstacle to modifying organizational behavior. If one seeks only to protect oneself, even if that protection is successful, growth and behavior change cannot result. When the wagons are drawn tightly into a circle, the only progress remotely possible is circular. The turtle is indeed safe when withdrawn into his shell, but he isn't going anywhere so long as he's there. So while he's remaining where he is, safe and sound, he is losing ground in whatever journey he had embarked upon.

One of the first steps in overcoming your emotional rejection of behavior change is to understand that change itself—of any nature—will be more beneficial than harmful. If this were not the case, the world would have ground to a screeching halt long ago. (Author and consultant Edgar Schein once remarked, "If you want to understand something, try to change it.")

Behavior change is even more difficult on the job. Training programs, incentive plans, and environmental changes can achieve short-term changes, but these are usually just "movements," not true self-perpetuating behavior changes. A salesperson might file his or her expense accounts on a timely basis if management threatens to delay reimbursement for late reports. But this doesn't really improve that salesperson's attention to detail in any other facet of the job, nor does it even guarantee continually responsible behavior in filing expense accounts. I once implemented a policy of delaying expense reimbursement for thirty days on every expense report over one week overdue. After three months, half my salespeople couldn't travel because their credit was exhausted and their expense reports were *still* delinquent. Guess whose behavior was changed quite quickly?

The reason short-term changes aren't very productive is that they weaken as time goes on, and they're seldom powerful enough to prevent relapses into old behavior—or worse, into behaviors that circumvent the incentive's aim while still gaining the incentive.

Organizational Land Mines

Why is behavior change often thwarted by organizational life? Here are the most common reasons:

1. *Organizations tend to treat people as if they were as interchangeable as equipment.* Hence, just as you might buy one type of oil for all the machinery, organizations often use one type of incentive or motivation for all employees. This is arrant nonsense. Some people's self-interest (the only long-term change agent) lies in recognition, others' in achievement, others' in power, and so on. Blanket motivational programs are as effective as blanket tax programs—they fail to recognize each individual's unique position.

2. *Peer pressure is powerful.* It can actually militate against specific behavior changes. Peers can create significant pressure not to "cave in" or "bend." Changing behavior is often seen as a capitulation by the individual, in the eyes of the peer group. Hence, the safety of conforming with group norms exerts inordinate pressure *not* to make individual changes.

3. *Activity and result are constantly confused.* For example, hotel personnel who have been asked to be more patient and courteous with guests in order to qualify for a "most courteous employee" award can overwhelm a weary traveler with information about amenities, recreation, the city, and their families—accompanied by a thousand reminders to "have a nice day"—without ever really caring about the guest at all. I don't know how many times I've received mediocre service from a guy who says, "Hi, I'm John, and I'm pleased to be your waiter tonight." The training and incentives behind most such behaviors consistently confuse activity—"have a nice day"—with results—a genuinely happy, well-cared for patron. As with the obtrusive waiter, the words and actions are often mistaken for the outcome. What do I, as the

manager, *really* want? Do I want loquacious waiters or happy customers? Talkative employees or increased sales? It's easy to focus on activity; after all, it's easy to monitor and short-term in nature. But it's difficult to focus on results, which are often long-term and more subjective. During the Civil War, General George B. McClellan molded a Union army that could drill, march, and look smartly "military." But it couldn't win battles. Ulysses S. Grant was much more lax about discipline and parade, but he knew how to use the army to defeat the Confederates. McClellan is a footnote in history, while Grant is a giant.

4. Behavior change must be internally generated. It is common knowledge among organizational sages that people will revert to what's most comfortable unless constant reinforcement (a fear, or pressure) is exerted. But this can also be understood as people returning to their "home base"—acting in those ways most congruent with their self-image. Such a tendency is the essence of self-consistency. The only way to truly change behavior, not just briefly move it, is to influence that self-perception through appeals to self-interest.

When I was in high school, an organization called the Lamplighters performed volunteer work at a charity organization home for blind children. It wasn't considered cool for guys to belong to the group, though they were desperately needed for the athletic activities and coaching. The Lamplighters' counselor recruited some of the school's most popular girls, in the hope of thereby attracting some of the boys for at least short-term help.

An interesting thing happended. A core group of boys—some athletes, some "eggheads," some near-hoodlums—not only took the bait but stayed with the program all year, even after some of the girls departed. They did so because the experience provided a tremendous boost to self-worth. All of us felt that something was being added to our image of ourselves. The "movement"—the allure of the girls—was replaced by *motivation.* The yearbook picture of the Lamplighters turned out to be a who's-who of the school.

5. Positive behavior changes (that is, those that contribute to the organization's goals and business direction) *are often punished.* Change demands trade-offs from both the organization and the individual. All too often, however, the manager who honestly and genuinely begins to show more assertiveness in reining in his department's spending is hauled on the carpet by a superior who patronizingly informs him or her that subordinates are complaining about the new constraints. "We don't like being treated like this," and, "We need more freedom," are calls that alarm the superior, who prefers a happy group, with no tremors of dissatisfaction. "Can't you gain the agreement of your people for these new cost controls?" the manager is asked.

The result of this equivocal attitude is continued free spending by resentful employees. Behavior change is like a transplanted flower—it need nurturing and personal care while it adjusts to its new circumstances.

6. Organizational systems often work against the desired behavior change. We worked with a major airline that was concerned about their counter agents being rude and short-tempered whenever they worked the later afternoon shift. The airline had invested considerable money in "human relations" training and "customer awareness" speakers, but still the complaints continued. Could we tell management why these stubborn agents refused to change their hostile behavior, despite the best efforts of the organization to show them the light?

Three days later we certainly could. It seemed that the late afternoon shift was "rush hour." Scores of flights left between 4:00 and 6:00 p.m. The trouble centered on passengers who were purchasing tickets at the counter with credit cards for which the agents couldn't get rapid authorizations.

When the agent's credit card validator said either "invalid" or "please call for verification," the airline's procedure required that the agent call the credit card authorization line, after checking a thick book of invalid and stolen cards. Phone lines were often busy—especially during rush hour—and the agent's customer line backed up. Unhappy, stalled customers would grumble and were often quite abusive when their turn finally came. No human relations training or employee-of-the-month contest could prevent these agents, quite understandably, from quickly losing their cool.

The behavior wasn't the problem, the *system* was. The airline was actually modifying behavior in the wrong direction. Systems have to support behavior change, not corrupt it. But whenever there seems to be a "communications breakdown," organizations are all too ready to blame their people rather than the structure within which their people must work.

We devised a procedure whereby a supervisor took all such credit card questions off to a separate line. The cardholders then felt that they were getting management attention for what was, 90 percent of the time, a computer glitch. The lines moved as they were designed to, and the agents got on with their jobs.

Flexibility

How good are you at behavior change? One indicator is in the test results from Chapter 1. The more your job behavior profile differs from your natural behavior profile for any given factor, the more potential flexibility you exhibit. But please note: the absence of such a difference doesn't necessarily imply a lack of flexibility— it could just mean that your successful job behaviors are a close match with your native behaviors, a condition that many people are fortunate enough to enjoy. (Another explanation would be that you simply refuse to change your "comfortable" behaviors, no matter what success at your job might actually require.)

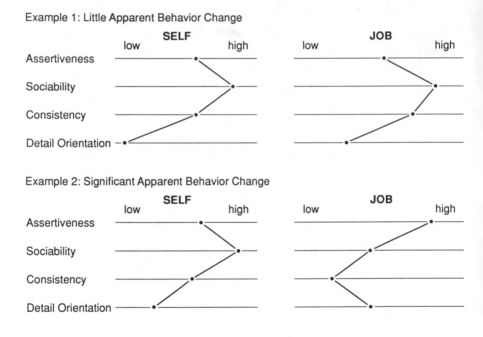

In example 1, the individual appears to slightly raise his or her assertiveness and consistency when on the job. However, on or off the job this is a people-oriented, sociable, verbal person with a low attention to detail. He or she may well be a creative, artistic, and charming person.

In the second example, the individual significantly raises assertiveness and attention to detail on the job, while lowering sociability and consistency. In this job role, the person will be a problem-solver and expediter who will move rapidly to get things done and may be seen as a "mover and shaker." He or she may or may

not work with and through people. The degree of people involvement will be almost exclusively determined by what is required
to meet goals and objectives. This person makes a substantial
adjustment in adopting the behaviors required by the job. Assuming that he or she is successful on the job, this represents significant flexibility and success at changing behavior. But this person
would almost certainly need a large battery to sustain such change
over the course of the working day.

Here's a quick test to measure your inclination toward behavior
change. Simply check yes or no about these statements, and be
as candid as possible.

	YES	NO	
1.	( )	( )	I find myself consciously exercising more patience with work colleagues than with people outside of work.
2.	( )	( )	Different people who know me well would describe me in substantially different ways.
3.	( )	( )	I am a person of relatively few surprises. Some people might call me predictable.
4.	( )	( )	Detail is detail, and I treat it the same whether it involves my tax return or vacation plans.
5.	( )	( )	I have the ability to turn the charm on and off.
6.	( )	( )	My ability to be assertive depends a lot on whether I'm on or off the job.
7.	( )	( )	My stress level is virtually the same on the job or off.
8.	( )	( )	My habits at the office are significantly different from those I have at home.
9.	( )	( )	My decision making tends to be either more cautious or more aggressive at work than it is on personal issues.
10.	( )	( )	There are certain types of people I tolerate equally poorly on the job and in social situations.

Here is the scoring key for responses that tend to show higher
flexibility.

	YES	NO
1.	(x)	( )
2.	(x)	( )
3.	( )	(x)
4.	( )	(x)
5.	(x)	( )
6.	(x)	( )
7.	( )	(x)
8.	(x)	( )
9.	(x)	( )
10.	( )	(x)

The test you just took isn't conclusive by any means. But if you chose the flexible responses seven times or more out of ten, you seem to be someone who can and does change behavior as required, *within whatever degree of change is available to you.* If your Chapter 1 test also shows flexibility (as in the comparison with the job inventory), then you have still another indicator of your willingness and ability to change. Remember, however, that willingness and ability are two different things. No matter how high the ability—the range within which you may adjust your behavior —the absence of willingness will result in inflexibility. Conversely, high willingness is of little benefit if your ability to change is limited. The latter situation is less of a problem, however, since virtually all of us possess at least a moderate potential to modify our behaviors.

Once you've begun to understand your own behavior, you can begin to better manage your relationships with others, as well as their relationships with each other. This is not manipulation— which implies the movement of people from hidden and ulterior motives—but rather, the effective management of people, their motivation, and their performance.

Miracle Cures Versus Real Help

How does one manage behavior effectively? One thing to avoid is the miracle cure, or latest management fad, be it est or firewalking. While living in California in the late 1970s, I was invited to attend an est overview session (est stands for Erhard Seminars Training, named after its founder, Werner Erhard). The est course was rather vociferously advocated by several friends who I thought had their acts together, so I agreed to attend the overview and listen to the ensuing sales pitch.

I found a zealous bunch of otherwise normal people who told me about the wonders of est. However, I learned that the est program itself couldn't be described. I had to experience it. In answer to the most rigorous questioning I could muster, the closest they could give me to a description was that est "would put me in touch with my own greatness." There was also the testimony of an apparently successful professional woman who told me, "I can now look people in the eye when they approach me on the street."

Now, two weekends of my life and several hundred dollars in cash might seem a small price to pay to get in touch with my greatness and learn how to look strangers in the eye, but I opted out. I did learn two things, though. First, selling something that can't be described but can only be appreciated by experiencing it is an awfully interesting marketing ploy. Second, there is tremendous power in the idea that people can achieve more when they understand themselves better, even when the means to understanding is offered in the form of "pop" pseudo-psychological experiences. The objective is valid, but beware of the means.

The last decade saw the rise and demise of est (it claims about half a million alumni), but the need it catered to remains strong. Erhard has begun a new program and derivative versions of it abound. One of the most intriguing of the crop is firewalking: participants, after varying degrees of preparation and exploration of their selves, apply what they've learned by walking barefoot over a bed of hot coals. The most striking thing about this approach to behavior change, in my opinion, is that it has apparently made a multimillionaire out of its young guru.

How much can any of these self-awareness experiences actually help an individual in an organizational environment? In the absence of any scientific data, I believe the 15–70–15 rule applies. Probably 15 percent of the participants do benefit from self-examination and sorting out their objectives, and many programs provide time for this. Another 70 percent will receive neither positive nor negative aftereffects, or will experience only a brief positive, or "halo," effect. The final 15 percent will be harmed because issues have surfaced without adequate resolution, or because a false sense of security has been engendered. Psychologists are already treating firewalkers who felt cheated when they found that the problems they face on the job cannot be conquered as easily as the bed of coals.

There are few greater powers in life than appreciating your talents and abilities, realizing how to apply them to solve problems effectively, and then making decisions correctly. This is an age-old human pursuit. So what is the best way to go about it?

People appear to perform at their best when they can use the full gamut of their talents and interests in their jobs. The more you're asked to use all of your skills on the job—and to stretch them beyond your current capabilities—the higher your morale will tend to be. The more you are discouraged from applying these talents, the greater your sense of unfulfillment. Many people probably turn to the pop psychologists and their work because of this basic malaise—they don't feel good about what they are doing, but they are not sure why.

Validated, reliable programs to determine underlying talents and provide recommendations on how to apply them are doing well and will continue to grow. This applies to company-administered testing, formal individual assessments, and independent, personal evaluations. A prime example of the last is the Johnson O'Connor Institute, now found in several major cities, where individuals can receive private, highly accurate, and sensitive feedback about personal traits and abilities. These approaches will persist long after firewalking is looked upon as a late 1980s fad.

It's uncertain whether the decade ahead will bring more extreme forms of the magic cures (perhaps sky diving without a parachute?) or more of an organizational approach to a very real problem. I suspect the latter will prevail, though the former will never disappear. There can be few pursuits more productive for the organization and for the individual than identifying and applying each person's basic talents in the correct job. Doing so will lead to a healthier workplace as well. And if I had to guess, we'd all be able to look each other in the eye a lot more easily.

Organizations don't manage people—other people do. And only through the cumulative best efforts of individuals are cultures established, goals met, and businesses driven forward. Since *every* business today is a people business, we'll now turn to the fundamental management skill of influencing others.

Notes

1. For example, see Marshall, MacLuhan, *Understanding Media: The Extensions of Man* (New York: McGraw-Hill, 1964).
2. David Wallechinsky, Irving Wallace, and Amy Wallace, *The Book of Lists* (New York: Bantam, 1978), pp. 469–470.

4

Management Influence: The Fine Art of Accommodation

Luck is the residue of design.
—Branch Rickey

Don't pity the martyrs, they love the work.
—George Ade

There are a finite number of behavioral styles that you can encounter during the daily course of your job. For example, here are two scenarios that could develop from the same circumstances: I am about to meet a potential customer—Mr. Riley—for the first time. I am meeting him at his office, and I've arrived ten minutes early for my scheduled 10:00 a.m. meeting. The receptionist calls him to announce my arrival.

Scenario 1.   At precisely 10:00 a.m., Riley's secretary appears to escort me to his office. Riley briefly shakes my hand, motions for me to sit across his desk from him, and asks if I'd like coffee, which his secretary will get for us. Once she leaves the room—which is nicely furnished, very utilitarian, and extremely orderly—Riley says, "What can I do for you?"

Scenario 2.   A minute or so after I'm announced, Riley appears in person, shakes my hand, and says, "Hi, I'm George Riley. Shall we go get some coffee?" He touches my arm to show me the way. After getting coffee, we return to his office, which is warmly furnished, with mementos and souvenirs on the walls and tabletops. Riley invites me to sit on a couch, and he sits nearby in a comfortable chair. He says to me. "So, tell me a little bit about yourself."

83

There could have been other scenarios, based on other dominant styles. Each requires a different kind of response. That is,
the person who wants to wield influence must make the required
adjustments. If you sail through life constantly expecting others
to adapt to you, you'll find that most people feel they have better things to do.

In scenario 1, Riley exhibits a high level of assertiveness and
a lower level of people orientation. He wastes no time and, being task-oriented, wants to know what I can provide to help him
meet his tasks and goals. If I try to engage him in small talk, he
would quickly grow restless (particularly if he has a low patience
level) and his interest and attention would wander. I should have
been able to quickly pick up these cues to his behavior by
evaluating his actions toward me and observing his office.

In scenario 2, Riley exhibits a very high people (or relationship)
orientation, higher than his task orientation. Consequently, he
wants to get to know me and to like me—and has to get *me* to
like *him*. Thus, we have to achieve a certain comfort level. If I
try to get down to business ("Let me tell you why I'm here") before
allowing Riley this familiarity, I would lose his interest and attention. Again, his predispositions should have been readily detect-
able through both his actions and his environment.

Adapting to Different Styles

We all walk into such circumstances every day, yet we are generally so caught up in our *own* behaviors—projecting the image
we create for ourselves—that we undermine such key encounters
through inadvertent self-centeredness. Whether we want to lead
subordinates, persuade the boss, influence colleagues, or convince customers, we must be prepared to adapt to their most comfortable style. Conversely, when you find yourself turned off by
a proposal, angry at a waste of your time, or threatened by more
closeness than you're used to, it's generally because others haven't
bothered to adjust to your most comfortable behavior.

In managing behavior successfully, you can use environmental cues and observed behavior to help determine the type of
person with whom you're interacting. (Being observant this way
is essential for salespeople, but it's also important for *anyone* wanting to influence others.) People who are considered natural
leaders are usually people who have developed the ability to
recognize these cues and behaviors.

Try to match up the observable behavior (what is said) and environmental cue with the related behavioral style:

Behavioral Style	Says	Behavior Observed or Environment
A. High task orientation	1. "Let's get on with it."	a. Nervous habits, constant movement
B. High detail orientation	2. "Good report but four typos."	b. Personalized, private "nest"
C. Low patience level	3. "How will this improve the status quo?"	c. Everything in its place
D. Low people orientation	4. "Let me try this on my own."	d. Functional, designed for effective work

(Answers below)

Of course, natural behavioral predispositions aren't always this obvious, and more study is sometimes required, as we'll discuss later in this chapter. But often behavior *can* be assessed this quickly if you have the discipline and inclination to do so. But here's a brief example of how *not* to do this.

A salesman—who was very people-oriented and highly sociable—made a call with me on a manager in a large government agency. The manager had files and reports neatly stacked all over the office and had markers in four colors aligned on his desk. He had been asking us only for statistics, references, and documentation. In a phrase, details were his life.

At precisely the time our meeting was to have ended, he concluded, "So, if you'll get me figures from other clients, separated by function, with the clients' comments underlined and your evaluation in the margins, I'll review them and let you know in two weeks." At which point my colleague decided to commit sales suicide and forced the *prospect* to adapt to *him*.

"We can do that, but why don't I tell you about our experiences and let you talk on the phone with some of our clients?"

"No, I'd prefer the report as I've laid it out."

"Okay, we'll send the report, but let me take another five minutes of your time and tell you about who we are and why we feel we're the best in our field."

"Well, my schedule is really rather full..."

I managed to get our salesman out before he insisted that the prospect take limbo lessons as well! How many sales opportunities had he blown through his refusal to recognize the client's predispositions and adapt to them?

Answers: A—3, d; B—2, c; C—1, a; D—4, b.

I'm a highly task-oriented person. I recall a representative of the San Francisco Chamber of Commerce visiting me when I managed a consulting operation in that city. I had already decided to join the Chamber before he sat down.

"Let me explain why your firm should join the Chamber."

"No need—I believe we should. How much is it, and whom do we pay?"

"Well, it's $400 per year, and here's the application and return envelope. Why don't I use the time to tell you what some of your membership privileges are."

"That's okay—my secretary will read the literature."

"All right. Then I'll explain who else belongs, and how the sub-committees operate."

"Look, I'm really very busy today. . ."

"But it will only take a few minutes."

He didn't know enough to stop when he had the sale! He was a relationship person who insisted on establishing a relationship even if it meant jeopardizing the sale (my getting annoyed) or endangering his health (my throttling him). Does this happen often? Every minute. Yet people keep themselves blithely ignorant of others' behavioral preferences. The underlying principle for managing behavior effectively is to take the time to recognize the behavioral predispositions of the people you're dealing with. Then act accordingly.

This brings us to flexibility, which is an essential component of adapting to others. In an earlier chapter, we asked, "At what price and for how long should behavior change?" Depending on battery size, we can change behavior either radically for a short time or moderately for a longer time, once we recognize which is needed.

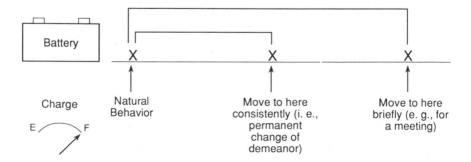

Perceptions and Labels

Our flexibility can also be affected by our perceptions of subordinates and by any labels we may have affixed to them. Here's just one example of how we tend to view subordinates:

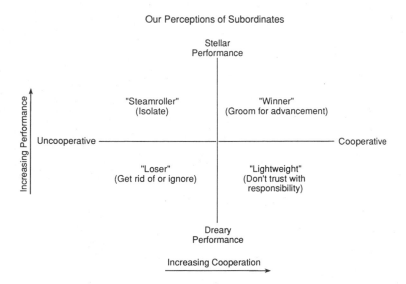

The differences among the people who have been labeled these ways are often not so great as they seem. But it's easier to categorize people than it is to try to understand them; once you've earned a label, it tends to stick like gum on hot pavement. You can't scrape it off. Our steamroller may simply need to develop some sensitivity to others' relationship needs. The lightweight probably needs more balance between task orientation and people orientation. The loser may be uncooperative *because* of poor performance. And the winner may simply be lucky in his or her current assignment.

All of these are suppositions, but they can easily be tested in reality. Labels, however, generally preclude such investigation.

To wield influence, managers must (a) understand their own behaviors (insight), (b) recognize others' behaviors (observations), (c) want to make the necessary adjustments in others' behavior (motivation), and (d) have the ability to make the necessary adjustments (flexibility). Here's a brief, simple, but effective guide to recognizing and evaluating your responses to others' behaviors:

Manager's Role	High Assertive	High Sociable	High Consistency	High Detail Orientation
Understanding others' desire for:	Results	Recognition	Consistency	Procedures
Enhancing others' flexibility by learning to:	Listen	Verify facts	Initiate	Make decisions
Help others conserve:	Time	Relationships	Acceptance	Accuracy
Support others':	Actions	Intuitions	Relationships	Principles
Answer this question:	What	Who	Why	How
Assist others' decision making through:	Options	Incentives	Guarantees	Evidence
Recognize others' need to be:	Efficient	Followed	Agreeable	Thorough
Provide this kind of supporting climate:	Free	Inspiring	Nurturing	Detailed
Understand and utilize others' special talents in:	Controlling	Socializing	Supporting	Precision

For example, subordinates you deem to be highly sociable as a dominant style (by listening to them and observing behavior and environment cues) will be best motivated if you provide recognition. Help them to build their relationships—the *worst* thing you could ever do would be to embarrass them in front of others. If they have a hunch, listen to it and provide serious feedback; (don't just ask them to come back with documentation). Utilize their knack for socializing to enhance morale, learn group sentiment, and gather grapevine news.

Look for your own predispositions on the previous chart, as well as those of your subordinates, colleagues, and superiors. Use it to make quick, simple adjustments to accommodate the needs of others as you seek to influence them. This is what the subtle art of persuasion is all about.

Making Adjustments: Fine-tuning

There are only three possible relationships between individual behaviors and those behaviors required by any given job:

1. There is a close or ideal fit, and no action is required regarding behaviors.
2. The fit is within reasonable bounds, but isn't tight; some adjustments are required on the part of the individual and/or the organization.
3. There isn't a good fit at all; no amount of adjustment will bring one about, so it's best to save the individual and the organization the grief of such a poor match.

To make such determinations, you must know the behaviors that a given job requires for successful completion and the native behaviors of any candidate for that job. But as you saw from Chapter 1's unscientific test, such determinations are well within our abilities to make. (If you took the test and completed the job inventory, you have both pieces of feedback already.)

Apart from self-tests and random observations, managers can do several things to determine how well their subordinates' behavioral styles compare with job demands:

1. Create comprehensive job descriptions. Every job description should cover the three elements we discussed earlier—physical ability, skills and knowledge, and behavioral needs—as specifically as possible. (For example, "incumbent must be comfortable with highly consistent and repetitive work since applications to be reviewed are 80 percent identical.")

2. Involve the employee. Openly discuss how the employee would structure his or her ideal job; listen for behavioral responses ("Every day would be different and diverse," or, "I'd like to be able to interact with others at will"). After two or three such conversations, you should be able to construct a fairly accurate behavioral profile.

3. Perform systematic observations. Note how an employee performs in highly detailed assignments and highly unstructured assignments. Become attuned to behavioral cues. (For instance, an employee consistently requests your presence whenever a particularly assertive vendor visits.) Over time—as little as thirty days—you should be able to discern a pattern for most people.

4. Compare notes with colleagues. Seek out the observations of others to ensure that you have feedback on an employee's behavior when you are not present. Do others' perceptions and observations support or negate your own? To what extent is *your* behavior the major influence on the behavioral style of the employee?

There are good reasons to understand how your behavior affects others' behavior. Here is just one quick example of how behaviors interact.

I once worked with a colleague named Gary. We were peers—each a vice president—and respected each other's opinions, abilities, and work. Consequently, I often went to Gary for advice. Our profiles would have looked something like this:

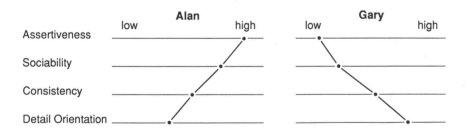

When I approached Gary, I would say, "Gary, I have three alternatives—A, B, and C. I'm leaning toward C, but I'd like your opinion." Gary would respond, "I agree with C—it's the obvious choice." On the next occasion, I would ask him, "Gary, I like proposition A, but what do you think about B and C?" And Gary would reply, "They just aren't as good as A."

After a while, I noticed two things: Gary never disagreed with me, and half my decisions weren't very effective. I finally caught on that my highly assertive style was inadvertently overwhelming Gary's analytic, low-key style to the point that he was agreeing with me, not on the basis of the facts, but on the basis of preserving the relationship. That's right—Gary was telling me what he thought I wanted to hear because he was very unassertive and I was highly assertive. Once I understood the dynamics of the behavioral relationship, the correction was simple.

"Gary," I'd say, "I have three alternatives, and I don't know which is best. What do you think?"

"Well, surely you favor one of them."

"Nope."

"Well, I'll go over them, and you can tell me any preference you develop."

After Gary was convinced that I was noncommittal, I got an honest, and very important response. It took only minor changes to adjust my behavior—any battery could have sustained it—but there was a world of difference in what I got back from Gary.

In how many of your relationships is the *form* distorting the *substance*? How often are you attributing the wrong causes to these natural behavioral discordancies? The four suggestions for managers listed above can help you minimize these discordancies.

The Eight Principles of Adaptation

Mastering the principles of adaptation is as essential a management skill as decision making or planning. Note that this is a skill; it is learnable, repeatable, and not dependent on a particular behavioral style. Highly assertive managers and unassertive managers can master these principles equally well.

1. Never use or accept labels to describe people. This is a pernicious habit that we unconsciously engage in all too frequently. In accepting labels—conservative, old, immature, steamroller, dense, nitpicker, and so on—we blind ourselves to both the potential of our employees and the technique available to us to modify and manage behavior.

> *Example:* You're about to begin a sales meeting and a colleague says to you, "Be careful if Carol speaks up. She's got a real chip on her shoulder." Ignore your colleague's advice.

2. *Listen carefully to what people say.*   If a colleague keeps saying, "All right, all right, but what's the point?" you're probably dealing with a highly assertive person who's afraid that time is being wasted. On the other hand, if you hear, "Let's slow down and list all these facts so we can analyze them carefully," you're dealing with a very detail-oriented person. Usually, we're too busy listening to *ourselves* to take the time to listen to these vital clues to the behavioral style of others.

> *Example:* A subordinate is doing poorly on a new assignment, and your boss suggests it's an "attitude problem." But as you listen to your subordinate, you hear, "Everything's so vague, the instructions seem contradictory, and I need more time to absorb everything." The "attitude problem" is more likely a case of a high-detail person needing more specific and better instructions from you.

3. *Observe the environment.*   An employee whose desk looks like it was struck by a typhoon every day is probably a safe candidate for low detail orientation. If your assistant always talks to employees about assignments at their work stations, as opposed to calling them into his or her office, your assistant is likely to be highly sociable.

> *Example:* You want to influence your assistant to be more assertive in demanding that deadlines be met. Are you going to do it by memo, a talk in your office, in a staff meeting—just how? You're probably best advised to do it casually in his or her office, or over a private lunch. (This might not be *your* most comfortable style, but it's your assistant's most comfortable style.)

4. *Observe and establish patterns of behavior.*   Over relatively brief time spans for daily colleagues—customers, vendors, and other outsiders take slightly longer—you can systematically construct behavioral style profiles. Does someone accept delegation better when explicit instructions are provided (high detail), or when they're told no more than, "Here's the goal—accomplish it in whatever manner you prefer" (low detail)? Does someone initiate contact with others and work to put them at ease (highly sociable), or interact only when approached and only about the task at hand (low sociability)?

> *Example:* You note over the course of four weekly staff meetings that your most competent technical rep never speaks out. You realize that her low-assertive, low-sociable behavior prevents others from sharing her experience and expertise. Consequently, you devise an approach wherein she submits a written report on product flaws, which you circulate prior to meetings, enabling people to ask her about her approaches.

5. Practice adapting on small issues first. If you're uncertain or uncomfortable in adapting to someone else's style, start on an inconsequential issue. Move forward gradually, until you are confident of (a) exactly what the other's most receptive style is, (b) what techniques would best cater to that style, and (c) your comfort level in using those techniques.

Example: You think Joe is a highly assertive person who prefers things cut-and-dried and without embellishment, but you're not certain. You'll need his enthusiastic support for the reorganization plan you're working on. So, in preparation, you approach him to get his advice on how this year's savings bond campaign should be run. You listen, observe, and develop a better understanding of Joe's behavior pattern as a result of his response to this (and perhaps other) minor issues.

6. Make your own style known. Most authorities believe that consistency, not a particular style, is the basis for effective leadership. And a great deal of employee discontent stems from the boss's unpredictability and inconsistency. You needn't issue memos about your style, but you can be frank and candid about what makes you most comfortable, even while in the process of adapting to others.

Example: A subordinate tells you that you don't seem to give his ideas proper consideration, and that he suspects you think he's too young to contribute anything. You respond that, aside from content—which you're always happy to critically discuss—he would help you (and his own cause) if he would document his suggestions in a certain format, instead of merely explaining them at staff meetings. You are better able to analyze things in writing, and if he could help you out, the entire process would be enhanced.

7. Make investment/return assessments. Your battery won't support radical behavior changes for unlimited periods. No one's will. How much energy do you have available? How much of a return are you willing to invest your energy for? You shouldn't adapt to everyone or every situation. What's the value to you?

Example: An important customer and a large supplier both insist on discussing new contracts over dinner whenever possible. You are uncomfortable with such socializing and resent the time taken from your family. It makes sense to invest your energy in a few cordial, supportive dinners with the client, who you can really commit yourself to, and to tell your supplier he'll have to see you in your office. It does not make sense to make a half-hearted attempt to accommodate both.

8. Discuss behavioral styles openly with colleagues.   Although we've provided techniques for individual use, adaptation is best accomplished when two people meet in the middle. This minimizes each person's discomfort, distance from native behavior, and energy investment. It also eliminates the uncertainty and hesitation that can result when you perceive that you are the *only* one making an effort to adapt!

> *Example:* You're with your boss, who says she doesn't see why you can't complete the design of the new sales training program in thirty days. You believe it will take at least ninety. Instead of a *content* debate, you suggest, "Look, you of all people know how detail-conscious and deliberate I like to be. And I know that, on principle, you want everything done yesterday! Why don't we agree on this: I'll report progress to you personally every Friday, and based on that, we should have a solid idea of a completion date after three reports. You can tell me if you think I'm overdoing the details and analyses, and I can tell you if you're tending to overlook key details. Agreed?"

If you are able to keep these eight principles in mind and use them *daily*—until they become as second nature as labeling and bias are for most people—you'll find yourself a far more effective leader and a much more efficient manager. It's all a question of adapting to others as smoothly and rapidly as possible.

Avoiding Quicksand

The best intentions and most carefully developed plans still run into plenty of trouble. The organization's processes, procedures, and culture are often the culprits. I call such traps "organizational quicksand" because, the more you struggle, the faster you sink. It's best to learn where the quicksand may await you so that, if possible, you can avoid the trap. Here are the most frequent forms of organizational quicksand that could undermine your attempts to manage and influence behavior.

Perceived Manipulation

People's perception sometimes is that they are being "used" by management. They tend to feel that they are deceived ("I don't believe we had a bad year—they just don't want to give salary increases"), shortchanged ("Sure, we get a 5 percent bonus, but the big shots must be getting at least 15 percent"), and/or wasted ("If there were any brains on the seventh floor, this would be a

Fortune 500 company"). Consequently, they will react very cautiously to your attempts to adapt to and influence them, sensing no possible good can come of it. How to convince them?

First, make certain that you're really *not* trying to manipulate anyone! Are you striving to increase the section's productivity, or are you trying to discourage legitimate vacations because you didn't plan properly? Employees are quick to discern these nuances and tend to never forget them. Second, if your objective *is* legitimate, be honest. Enlist their help, "Look, we need field sales projections analyzed and consolidated in three days instead of four this month for the board meeting. I'll relax my insistence that all backup data be in a single format (high detail) and won't ask you every hour what your progress is (high assertive). In return, can we agree on a shorter deadline with minimum disruption?"

Such methods are far superior to memo and fiat; you're attempting to be honest about the actual situation before perceptions of manipulation can take root. But you must be consistent, honest, and receptive in situations where perceived manipulation is likely. Employees will only give you one shot. After that, your credibility will disappear with your map, and it's into the quicksand.

Political Realities

Anytime two or more people assemble, a political dynamic is present. That fact is neither good nor bad, but it does have consequences. Organizational politics involves issues such as ego, turf, status, leverage, power, and the like. Politics is the natural condition of reconciling conflicting and competing interests for the common good.[1] Political reality is natural, unavoidable, and healthy. Yet we continually hear cries of, "It's politics," "It's the system," and, "It's not what you know, it's who you know."

Political quicksand can engulf you when your attempt to change behaviors—whether yours or that of others—is seen as not being for the common good, that is, as an attempt to foster purely personal interests, private benefits, and /or singular status. (Note that "manipulation" is usually attributed to "them" and "the powers that be," while individuals are seen as engaging in "politics.")

To accommodate political realities, you must rely heavily on the fundamental change agent we discussed earlier—rational self-interest. Demonstrate how the behavior change will make the job easier and/or better: "Look, we need to exercise more patience (high consistency) and follow-through (high detail) with customer complaints taken over the phone. Whenever customers are unhappy with our hurried or incomplete response, they write a letter to the president, and his office demands three times the response details we'd have to give if we took our time with the original call. If we cut presidential complaints by even one-third, we'd practically eliminate these ten-hour days."

Of course, you'll look great if you're successful in modifying behavior to provide better responses to complaints. But that's not the main point. Success is gained by approaching this not as a political issue, but as a matter of self-interest for everyone.

Cultural Immune Systems

Every organization has a cultural "immune system" that tends to reject foreign incursions—be they people, ideas, or approaches. The organization's culture will also tend to reinforce and perpetuate the core belief systems of the organization—for better or worse.

Don't struggle against company culture. You'll only sink faster and deeper if you do. But don't ignore it either. A culture that says, "Do it this way because we've *always* done it this way," won't allow you to manage and change behaviors without great difficulty.

Establish your own mini-culture. The larger the organization, ironically, the easier this is, because it's easier to create a corner for yourself that is invisible to the larger view. Do this by demonstrating and exemplifying that, in your area, new ideas *do* count and *will* be acted on. Show your willingness to adapt your behaviors, and encourage your subordinates to follow suit. You're not "spitting into the wind" if you can establish a unit whose productivity and performance reflect the benefits of managing behavioral styles.

For example, if you find that the organization frowns upon innovation (high assertive and low consistency), take your people off-site for a meeting about how to be more creative in your environment. If the organization favors little socialization but you feel you must achieve greater team-building (high sociability), begin to work with people at their desks, in their offices, and at meetings in common areas. Remember, people react to what they see, not what they hear, and you're quite capable of creating a mini-culture based on the example you set—the way in which you manage your own behaviors.

These techniques can be useful in avoiding organizational quicksand (or, at least, in extricating yourself from it if you can't avoid it). In the next chapter, we'll examine ways in which you can proactively manage daily routines, using your understanding of behaviors to reach new levels of excellence. So now that we've avoided the pitfalls, let's scale the heights.

Note

1. See Alan Weiss, *Surviving and Succeeding in the Political Organization* (New York: AMACOM, 1978).

5

Peak Performance Results: Managing Behavior at Work

80 percent of success is just showing up.
—Woody Allen

Woody Allen's dictum is from another age. Today, it's all too common to hear a manager moan something like this, "It's a pity—Joe was my best underwriter, but he retired five years ago when he felt he had reached a dead end in his advancement here."

"Too bad. Do you miss him?"

"Miss him? He's right over there at his desk!"

There are discrete management issues that require the application of management skills in behavior change. Let's examine what they are and how to approach them.

Conflict and Confrontation

It has been our experience that behavioral issues sometimes constitute the lion's share of management difficulties. Conflict, for example, is often attributed to "personality differences" or "poor chemistry" or a "breakdown in communications." These factors account for conflict in perhaps one percent of all situations. Conflict is most often the result of one of two things: disagreement over goals, or over ways to achieve them.

In conflicts over goals, there's a need to clarify who owns the decision (who will be held accountable for its outcome), and whether there is basic agreement on essential objectives (musts) as opposed to nonessential objectives (desires). Disagreement about objectives is usually *strategic* disagreement: for example, a difference of opinion over whether to pursue an increase in market share or an increase in profitability. (Personally, it could be the strategic question about having children: whether to be a full-time mother or to pursue a career again as soon as possible.) Conflict about goals requires both objective and subjective communication and evaluation among the interested parties, based on the key recognition that it's the end result that's important.

Conflict about ways to achieve goals, however, is usually tactical and operational in nature and can occur even when there's agreement about the goals. To pursue an increase in market share, you can add to the sales force, increase advertising, cut prices, and so on. To have a child and pursue a career, you can utilize day care, grandparents, a brief sabbatical, a househusband, and so on. Conflict about these options is usually best worked out through logical, empirical analysis of the facts as they relate to both reward and risk. Those most affected by the goal should play a key role in analyzing alternative methods to achieve it and in deciding which one to use.

Which of these individuals will tend to react best to confrontation over goals?

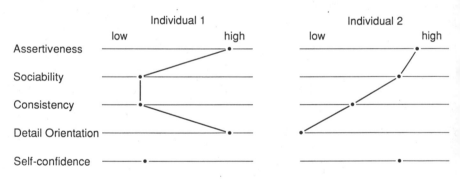

Individual 1 tends to be indecisive (assertiveness and detail are equally high), somewhat tense (consistency is significantly lower than detail orientation), highly methodical (high detail), assertive, and somewhat low in self-confidence, with low sociability. The second individual is firm, sociable, moderately consistent, comfortable with ambiguity (low detail), and very self-confident. If I were in a debate about goals, I'd certainly prefer to deal with the second person, who would tend to be more effective at dealing with conflict.

But does this mean that the first individual is doomed to poor decisions and perpetual hostilities? Not at all—this is where flexibility and change in behavior play a key role. The ability of this person to use effective change agents to modify behavior for the duration of a particular conflict will largely determine his or her success.

Managers can intervene by abetting such behavior changes for as long as needed to resolve a conflict. By using the change agent already cited—rational self-interest—and the techniques we describe below, the manager can effect the changes in Individual 1 illustrated below.

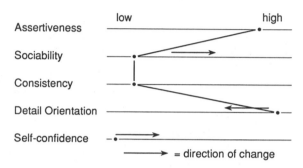

Individual 1—
Behavior Modified for Conflict Resolution

Conflict Resolution

Conflict resolution is a healthy, essential management activity. It requires, however, appropriate behaviors, some of which you can deliberately modify to achieve such resolution, provided that:

1. You recognize the conflict situation;
2. You are aware of your current behaviors;
3. You know the behaviors that are more effective in resolving the conflict;
4. You want to make any necessary adjustments; and
5. You are capable (have the battery and flexibility) to make those adjustments.

This is a simple process, but one requiring management attention and scrutiny. Conflict is healthy when it is intelligently managed. It is deadly when it is left to chance and random behaviors.

Relationships, in general, can be quite confounding unless the behavioral underpinning is understood. Here's a common example:

You and I hold opposite positions on an issue. We are both highly assertive people with little need to please others. We are expediters—"movers and shakers." Our profiles look like this:

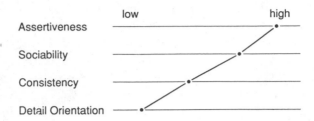

Our mutual superior is an easy-going, amiable person who prizes relationships—including those with subordinates. He has a fine record as a manager and believes in careful consensus-building, not making threats, and nurturing employees. He dislikes confrontation and places paramount importance on being liked and accepted by others. His profile looks like this:

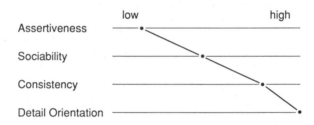

You enter his office, explain your sentiments and insist, "There's only one sensible course of action, and it's yes, yes, yes, yes, yes!" To which he replies, "You certainly have a logical position, and I appreciate it."

Later I go to see the boss and emphatically stress that the only way to go is "no, no, no, no, no!" And he responds, "I can see why you feel that way, and I understand the reasoning."

Still later, you and I meet in the hall, equally smug. "Well, I guess we know what we'll be doing," you say. "We certainly do," I reply, "It's 'no, no, no, no, no,' and the boss agrees completely!"

"What are you talking about, liar," you gently answer, "He said he agreed to 'yes, yes, yes, yes, yes!'"

And then we both think:

"You're lying."

"You've distorted the facts."

And:

"The boss is wishy-washy."

"He's a wimp."

"His favorite color is plaid."

What happens if both of us confront the boss with his alleged perfidy? He says, "Look, I'm the one who will decide, and I heard you both out because I respect you both. But I didn't say I agreed with either of you, and don't try to pressure me to act before I'm ready. I'll decide what's right after I do some further checking, and not a minute sooner."

The boss is still trying to preserve relationships, but his assertiveness has been forced up by our impudence. In how many instances, every day, do we misconstrue, misinterpret, and mistake the actions of our colleagues, basing our perceptions on "motives" and "hidden agendas" that don't actually exist at all?

Too often. And to compound the error, we seek justifications in all kinds of irrelevancies: gender, education, beliefs, background, age, associations, reputation, rumor, and so on. We destroy communication—and worse, relationships—because we don't take the time to understand the behavioral basis for communication and relationships.

To resolve conflict, the manager must:

- Recognize subordinates' styles and separate them from content.
- Deal with the message and its delivery as separate issues.
- In so doing, reduce the stress levels.

The subordinate must:

- Recognize the style that the boss is most receptive to.
- Adjust his or her delivery to match that style.
- In so doing, reduce the stress levels.

Decision Making

Decision making is one of the most common of all management activities. There are systems and methodologies of decision making that any of us can use, despite behavioral predispositions. But no matter how eminently sensible and applicable a system of management may seem in a classroom or during a seminar, how, when, and even if, we choose to apply it will be largely determined by our behavioral predispositions. Course designers have labored for decades trying to determine how to "transfer" skills back to the job, but they have been working in the dark so long as they have omitted human behavior from their equations. A superb guitarist who is left-handed cannot use a right-handed guitar, no matter how well it is constructed. Similarly, the best decision making system in the world will not be adopted by someone who finds its methods in conflict with his or her behavioral orientation. For example, we have consistently observed managers with a low tolerance for detail struggle with—

and even deliberately fudge the facts on—decision matrices that require exhaustive collection and analyses of data. They would rather go with their intuition and fix whatever goes wrong later.

To give you an idea of behavioral decision-making style, look first at assertiveness and detail orientation scores. While there are other variables to consider, these two factors can give you a quick view of the way in which you tend to make decisions under most conditions. There are three basic possibilities.

The "Damn the Torpedoes" Risk-Taker.   At the Battle of Mobile Bay, Union Admiral David Farragut shouted his immortal order when informed of Confederate mines: "Damn the torpedoes, full speed ahead!" At the time, Farragut was lashed to the mast of his flagship, the *Brooklyn,* high above the water. It is not recorded what the sailors at the waterline, staring at the mine, had to say.

Farragut's assertiveness score would have been much higher than his detail orientation score. This combination represents a person who is a relatively aggressive decision maker and who will tend to be proactive rather than reactive. Risk-taking will be acceptable, and intuition and gut-level feelings will be accommodated. This firm decision maker will take responsibility for decisions and would rather take action today when 95 percent confident than wait for tomorrow to be 98 percent confident. He or she will take action, understanding that one can move quickly to correct anything that goes wrong as the decision unfolds.

The higher the assertiveness scores and the lower the detail orientation scores, the more pronounced these traits will be. The scores above show a highly aggressive, "damn the torpedoes" decision maker who will tend to be bold, confident, and assertive, accepting high levels of risk if the potential benefits seem to justify it.

The "Don't Do Anything Until We're 100 Percent Certain" Decision Maker. This profile represents analytic, calm, and careful decision makers. They prefer to crunch the numbers and digest all the data before committing to a course of action. They can be as forceful and firm as the risk-taking decision makers, but only after they are confident that they have all the facts and have examined all the options. These people do not like to be rushed or hurried and will gladly wait the extra day to increase their certainty. Colleagues will be asked, "What evidence do you have?" and, "Why do you say that?" and, "Where is the support?" They are trying to generate only reliable and justified information. Intuition, hunches, and "what feels good" will seldom influence this decision maker. Risk will not be tolerated unless there is evidence that it can be controlled. Generally, these decision makers will settle for less benefit in return for less risk.

The lower the assertiveness score and the higher the detail orientation scores the more conservative this person will be. The scores above show an extremely conservative, cautious, and risk-averse individual who will move only at his or her own speed and only with the confidence that all information is present and understood.

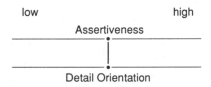

Decision Making Under Internal Conflict. When the assertiveness score and the detail-oriented score are about the same—the line connecting them would be nearly vertical—the decision maker is indecisive. This person will seem to vacillate in making decisions and may well change his or her mind several times before finally committing to a course of action. There are clear behavioral reasons for this, yet we often dismiss these people as "wishy-washy," "political," and even "cowardly." Let's take a more dispassionate look from the standpoint of these two simple behavioral relationships.

Risk-taking decision makers are usually aggressive because their assertive tendencies are stronger than their need to analyze detail, conform with authority, go by the book, or seek approval (all traits related to detail orientation). The reverse is true for conservative decision makers: these people have more of a need to conform, study details, and follow precedent than they do to act immediately and assertively.

But for our third kind of decision maker, these two factors are in direct conflict. That is, the behavioral urge to take action and to get on with it is counterbalanced by the need to make sure all information has been amassed, assimilated, and evaluated. The willingness to take risk is offset by the desire to avoid risk (or, at least, to control it). The result of this decision-making conflict is indecision. This decision maker will often make several, often conflicting, decisions, trying to work each one through. The attempt to work out this internal conflict is seen externally as vacillation and procrastination. Labeling such behavior with emotional terms such as "wishy-washy" or "political" helps nothing; but trying to help this decision maker resolve the conflict will produce positive results.

Finally, this direct conflict between assertiveness and detail orientation can be an indicator of uncertainty or confusion about one's job, position, and/or responsibilities. Clarifying these issues can often resolve the conflict and enable the decision maker to function more decisively. It is fairly common to see this vertical-line relationship in those who are newly appointed to a position, or who are in a position around which conditions have abruptly and significantly changed—in other words, the old rules no longer apply.

Decision making is just one management activity that can be objectively examined and perhaps better understood by looking at the behavioral underpinnings. All we've done is look at the relationship between assertiveness and detail orientation and draw some logical conclusions. This avoids the emotional, hysterical, or inflammatory attitudes that can get in the way of sound management and healthy interpersonal relationships.

The other two factors—sociability and consistency—will also influence the decision making profile of the individual. What would the difference be in the decision making of the following two individuals?

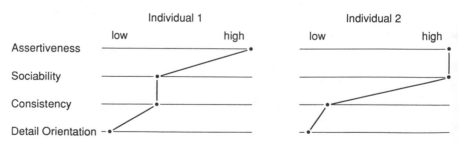

These individuals are both assertive, risk-taking decision makers—their assertiveness is significantly higher than their detail orientation. They have identical consistency levels, but individual 1 will tend to make solitary decisions, not needing the input of others unless they have vital information not available to him or her. Individual 2, on the other hand, will attempt to involve others and will prefer to build some consensus, actively eliciting the opinions of others. The difference between the two can be seen in their sociability scores.

By studying profiles in a holistic manner—looking at the gestalt, if you will—we can develop a comprehensive understanding of how an individual is prone to act in any variety of situations. This behavioral profile is a far better indicator of future behavior than is past performance.

Stress

> Worry often gives a small thing a big shadow.
> —Swedish proverb

In the profile, stress is a function of the relationship between consistency and detail orientation. Stress is generally present the more a low tolerance for consistency (impatience) is combined with a high tolerance for detail and need for structure.

From a behavioral standpoint, we're saying that the more your need to "get on with it" is thrown into turmoil by your relatively high need to "do it by the book," conform, and please authority, the more this particular conflict will create internal stress. In fact, stress is virtually inevitable in people who are basically impatient, yet forced by their own predispositions to wait until all the facts are in, until superiors have approved, until everything is "just right."

Internal conflict is a primary cause of stress, the external symptoms of which are often misunderstood—"You get much too nervous about these contracts. Maybe you should ask for more help." The additional help, of course, would make no difference whatsoever. Stress is another conflict that calls for intelligent management and can begin with the individual. Stress is as likely to be self-induced by such conflicting predispositions as it is to be environmentally induced. Health clubs and exercise are, at best, adaptive actions aimed at treating the symptoms. To achieve *real* health, the cause must be addressed. You must become aware of what generates your internal stress so that it can be ameliorated through different approaches to, and expectations from, work.

The degree of change possible—and the degree of change to be managed—in reducing stress is a function of what I call the "rubber band dynamic." If you place a rubber band on a table and leave it alone, it would, theoretically, stay that way for whatever time it took for the rubber to eventually decompose— perhaps a decade, a century, or an eon. However, if you stretch the rubber back tautly between your hands, then twist it, it will snap in much shorter order.

The same is true of behaviors. Left to your own devices, with no pressure or motivation or requirement to change, your behavior will remain constant and will not produce stress (other than the amount normal to your behavioral set). Once change is required, however—to achieve goals, to meet aspirations, to conform, for whatever reason—two factors will determine the added stress level.

- How much change? Is a modest change required, for a short period, or a substantial change for a prolonged period?

- At what cost? How big is the battery that must support the change and invest the energy necessary to accomplish it?

Here are two circumstances—deliberately placed at extremes— that demonstrate responses to these questions. In the first case, the change is moderate and easily supported. In the second, it is extreme and poorly supported.

Example 1: Low stress change (large battery, moderate movement)

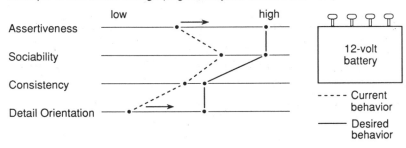

Example 2: High stress change (small battery, substantial movement)

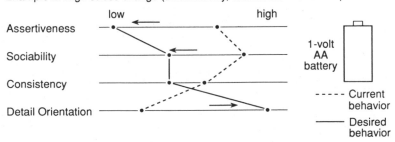

In example 1, a high-energy sales manager is required to raise her assertiveness and attention to detail slightly during one-hour, daily staff meetings. The adjustment is easily accomplished and is not stressful. In example 2, the same sales manager is asked to substantially lower assertiveness, somewhat lower sociability, and significantly raise detail orientation because she has been promoted to assistant sales director, a post in which she is expected to give administrative, very detail-oriented assistance to the director. Even a large battery would be depleted attempting to support this change day in and day out during a 40- or 50-hour week. Relying on a small battery would result in very high stress levels.

Stress and the Middle Manager

The likelihood of such stress affecting managers is increasing exponentially. Over the past several years, middle management ranks have shrunk by 15 percent in the United States, and the trend is guaranteed to continue—for these reasons, among others:

- The emphasis on higher productivity, which makes the middle manager a highly vulnerable target, with little direct impact on productivity but with clear salary and benefit cost considerations

- A general sentiment that staffs have been allowed to grow too large, too removed, and too inefficient, and that replacing them, even in boom times, will not add to profitability

- A trend toward the more participatory organization, with greater communication, in which a multitude of management layers are anathema

- The new technologies, which, among other things, reduce the need to employ cadres of managers to gather, interpret, and relay data

Experts estimate that more than one million middle-management jobs have been eliminated in the past decade. From 1982 to 1988, Mobil has cut white-collar jobs by 17 percent, DuPont by 15 percent, and GE Medical Systems by 35 percent. We are accustomed to reading about the blue-collar steel mill worker who can't be retrained to learn data processing. But what about the $40,000, 20-year administrative services manager at an insurance company who has become redundant or obsolete? Prudential Insurance, a conservative, paternalistic employer that had not laid off an employee in its 150-year history, including the depression years, in the 1980s has laid off about 1,500 people, many of them middle-management. Why? Because Prudential sees the move as absolutely critical if it is to remain competitive in the years ahead.

Firms are learning that they can "do without," or at least with fewer managers. Consequently, there is a greatly heightened level of stress and tension among remaining management personnel, owing largely to the demands that they be more adaptive behaviorally than ever before.

In a survey conducted by D'Arcy Masius Benton & Bowles, the most frequently cited source of stress was "not doing the kind of work I wanted to"; the second most frequent response was "coping with the current job."[2] Thus, stress, one of the five most critical threats to American health, according to the U.S. Department of Health,[3] is probably most often caused by poor job fit, inability to get along with others, and an inability to cope in general.

Stress may be psychological, physical, or both. Absenteeism, heavy drinking, substance abuse, spouse abuse, minor pains, and overeating, for example, are often attributed to other causes but are likely to be the venting of stress. Ninety percent of administrative and clerical respondents to another poll cited absenteeism as their most common response to stress. Middle and senior-level managers, however, reported that they channel stress into interpersonal difficulties (90 percent) and psychological problems (75 percent)[4]. About 63 percent of middle managers react to stress with substance abuse. In yet another poll, 83 percent of all respondents reported that at least *half* of all stress-related behavior goes undetected by employers.[5]

The costs of stress to the individual and the organization are immense. For example, stress-related disability claims cost organizations twice as much as physical claims ($8,000 verus $4,000 average per employee), and they account for an increasing number of claims—now over 15 percent (up from 5 percent in 1980).[6] The cost of such stress-related problems is enormous: it is estimated by health insurers—in terms of claims, lost productivity, and related expenses— at $150 *billion* annually.[7] The Center for Disease Control projects that the situation will get worse and will add to the number of cases of neurosis disorder, anxiety, drug abuse, sleep difficulty, and other physical ailments.[8] In 1988, the American Institute of Stress estimated that about 500 companies had "stress management" programs, a fivefold increase over the previous five years.[9]

It is apparent that the development of human resources in the 1990s will require a holistic view. Productivity and innovation will depend as much on a manager's psychological and physiological well-being as they will on job design, skill training, and rewards.

Stress Prevention

There is ample evidence that the demands on managers to change their behaviors will intensify substantially. Owing to increasing pressures on their own jobs, managers' stress levels are soaring. But coping with one's *own* stress is a prerequisite to helping subordinates deal with theirs. And the key to this is *prevention*, not what has unfortunately come to be called "stress management." I say "unfortunately" because the notion that stress should be managed rather than prevented is a key failing of most "wellness" programs (another dreadful term) and of most organizations' stress management programs. This is like opting for tooth decay "management" rather than dental hygiene. (The dentistry profession accomplished a major reorientation a decade or so ago when it consciously shifted its emphasis from better ways to fill and replace teeth to better ways to prevent tooth decay and periodontal diseases.)

The three most stressful jobs in America, according to one perhaps half-facetious poll, are:

1. Being a policeman working in the South Bronx between 8:00 p.m. and 4:00 a.m.
2. Being a window washer working above the twelfth floor on a skyscraper in the winter in a city north of 41° latitude.
3. Being a deckhand on a gasoline barge on the Mississippi River during a foggy night in New Orleans.[10]

Perhaps you have your own candidates for this list. I know my wife would nominate raising teenage children, and a friend suggests the "job" of rooting for the New York Giants.

But these jobs are all stressful because of environmental factors. There are many other causes of stress: financial pressure, peer pressure, real health concerns, crises, trauma, and so on. Most stress—particularly job-related stress—is self-imposed or organizationally imposed as a result of poor behavioral compatibility between either you and your job or you and your coworkers, customers, vendors, and so on.

I conducted an informal poll among executives, entrepreneurs, business school deans, and others, asking them to name the major training needs they perceived for the remainder of the 1980s. I provided no choices, yet four answers dominated all others—leadership skills, negotiation skills, sales training, and stress management.

The importance of helping managers deal with stress seems to be borne out by what's occurring in the work environment. Organizations that put in corporate gyms, pools, and running tracks still have them. These weren't transient employee benefits or frills that disappeared in the recession along with first-class travel and limousines. The gyms are still there, and they are being used, sometimes manditorily. Moreover, firms are offering a staggering variety of fitness and wellness programs that address the whole person. Finally, we see a rising number of employee assistance programs (EAPs) that offer help in areas such as divorce, drug addiction, and alcohol abuse. In 1959 there were only fifty such programs in the United States; today there are thousands.

The management and alleviation of stress require work on the part of both employees and organizations. Perhaps the first step for both parties is to understand those elements in the changing workplace that intensify stress for managers. Among them are the following:

- The line between manager and worker is increasingly vague. The traditional manager's position has been weakened by the cutbacks and by general criticisms caused by the last economic downturn.

- Even routine business events are now influenced by a global marketplace and a complex economic system. These are new and confusing factors that management has not been trained to handle.

- The two-career family has created vastly different personal pressures, especially when children are present. There are few role models or precedents to follow since this is the first generation coping with these pressures.

- Intellectual responsibilities are more demanding than ever. The key management roles emerging are those of decision maker and consensus-builder. Moreover, managers must also perform as team leaders, helping others to manage the stressful parts of *their* jobs as well.

- The telecommunications revolution has increased the pace of business and the information load. With instant access to vast amounts of data, managers must make rapid, high-quality decisions of major import.

- There is a prevailing idea in today's workplaces that if we take some quiet, peaceful time to ourselves (precisely what's needed to alleviate stress), we will be losing ground at work. Working long hours has come to be exepcted—the rule, not the exception, for top performers.

Stress Indicator Test

Here is a self-test to determine your stress level at work, followed by some techniques to use on yourself or with subordinates to help to alleviate stress. However, remember that the *best* technique is to *prevent* stress before it occurs on the job by aligning personal behaviors with job behaviors to achieve job compatibility. You don't want to manage a boat sinking, you want to prevent it from sinking. This is especially important if stress is a factor in your personal profile already.

STRESS INDICATOR TEST

Check the appropriate box:	Always	Sometimes	Never
1. I find myself yelling at subordinates.	[ ]	[ ]	[ ]
2. I am impatient.	[ ]	[ ]	[ ]
3. It seems like things are never done exactly right.	[ ]	[ ]	[ ]
4. Certain personalities immediately put me on edge.	[ ]	[ ]	[ ]
5. Certain issues immediately put me on edge.	[ ]	[ ]	[ ]
6. I haven't sufficient time to meet deadlines.	[ ]	[ ]	[ ]
7. I'm missing important information on details.	[ ]	[ ]	[ ]
8. I'm uneasy and can't identify the cause.	[ ]	[ ]	[ ]
9. My job is uninteresting and unchallenging.	[ ]	[ ]	[ ]
10. I'm worn out at the end of the day.	[ ]	[ ]	[ ]
11. Procedures and policies hinder more than help.	[ ]	[ ]	[ ]
12. It's difficult to really please my boss.	[ ]	[ ]	[ ]
13. I'm uncertain of what's expected of me.	[ ]	[ ]	[ ]
14. My career seems stalled or at a dead end.	[ ]	[ ]	[ ]
15. It's difficult to communicate with some of my colleagues.	[ ]	[ ]	[ ]
16. I am called too stubborn or too assertive or uncaring.	[ ]	[ ]	[ ]
17. Looking out for myself is the best way to succeed.	[ ]	[ ]	[ ]
18. I am indecisive owing to circumstances around me.	[ ]	[ ]	[ ]
19. My true talents are not completely utilized.	[ ]	[ ]	[ ]
20. My interests in life do not arise in my work.	[ ]	[ ]	[ ]

Scoring: Allow three points for each "Always," one point for each "Sometimes," and no points for each "Never."

Interpretation:

0-15:	You tend to handle stress extremely well, and there's a high probability that your behaviors are extremely compatible with those required for success in your job. You don't let stress affect you.
16-30:	You tend to manage stress competently. Stress that you can't prevent, you deal with effectively in most instances. Your job is probably a fairly good match with your natural predispositions.
31-45:	You are stressed to the point that it is affecting your performance in some manner and, at the high end of the score, your personal life and/or health as well. You are not preventing stress and are managing it ineffectively. You may well be unhappy in a job that is not compatible with your native behaviors.
46-50:	Your stress level is probably causing serious work, personal, and/or health problems. You are neither preventing nor managing stress-- it is controlling you. Your job is probably incompatible with your natural behaviors.

Low Stress			*High Stress*
0-15	16-30	31-45	46-50
(pleasure)	(comfort)	(discomfort)	(misery)

Stress Reduction

Stress prevention, while the most desirable method for dealing with stress, is not always possible, no more than our ability to always prevent fires, tooth decay, or marital disputes, despite our best efforts. This is particularly true as we proceed up the career track, change jobs, relocate, have children, mature, and go through other inevitable life changes. Here is one technique for dealing with stress—the stress separation technique—that is helpful in *reducing* stress through your own efforts.

The Stress Separation Technique

I. List below all those issues that are currently causing you stress (that is, those issues that made you check "Always" or "Sometimes" on the Stress Indicator Test).
  Examples:

1. My performance evaluations are two months overdue.
2. I wasn't selected for a highly visible task force assignment.
3. My best salesperson's spouse is terminally ill.

1. _____

2. _____

3. _____

4. _____

5. _____

6. _____

7. _____

8. _____

9. _____

10. _____

II. Review the above list, and write below those issues that clearly can be resolved through direct action. List the issues and actions below.

Example:

Issue: My performance evaluations are two months overdue.

Action: Come in thirty minutes early and complete two every morning for six days.

Issue	*Direct Action*
1. _____	1. _____
2. _____	2. _____
3. _____	3. _____
4. _____	4. _____
5. _____	5. _____

III. Review the items from the original list not dealt with in Part II. List below those stress issues that require more information.

That is, you might be able to include them in Part II if you were sure of the cause.

Example:

Issue: I wasn't selected for a highly visible task force assignment.
Clarification: Why wasn't I? Who made the selection?

Issue	*Clarification Needed*
1. _____	1. _____
2. _____	2. _____
3. _____	3. _____
4. _____	4. _____
5. _____	5. _____

IV. Now review the items from the original list that weren't included in Parts II or III. These are the issues that can't be reconciled through action or clarification on your part. They require a change in your philosophy or attitude.

Example:

Issue: My best salesperson's spouse is terminally ill.
Philosophic adjustment: My sales problems from his absence pale in comparison to *his* loss. I'm the fortunate one.

Issue	*Philosophic Adjustment*
1. _____	1. _____
2. _____	2. _____
3. _____	3. _____
4. _____	4. _____
5. _____	5. _____

The stress separation technique is my favorite because it is quite simple and it is self-controlled. But there are many such methods. The key to effective stress management is to make the items visible, separate them by category, then *act* on those you can and *adjust* to those on which you can't take action. And do this every day,

as a morning or evening discipline, so that you are acting to alleviate your stress level. You can refer to the lists—they should be
kept in your personal diary, calendar, appointment book, or wallet
—whenever you feel anxious without really understanding why.

In conclusion, effectively managing behavior requires you to
manage your own as well as that of others. Learn to modify and
adapt your behavior so that you can remove that onus from
others. In doing so, you'll find that preventing stress is readily
accomplished. At the very least, you'll have techniques at your
disposal to effectively deal with unavoidable stress.

Stress and the Permanent "Bad Day": Misinterpreting Behaviors

We've all experienced the surly salesperson, the uncooperative
telephone operator, and the indecisive manager. We often attribute
such unacceptable and unproductive behavior to a "bad day," but
sometimes something much more basic is going on: these are
people who have been forced into roles that don't suit their natural
behavior, and their "misbehavior" is an expression of their frustration. Stress management is such a hot topic today because of the
internal roll that such mismatches create.

Here are some examples of behavior that you've probably
observed during the course of a typical business week. These
behaviors can cause you stress, uncertainty, and a loss of productivity if you receive them emotionally. But if you can see them
as behavioral responses, you can deal with them more effectively—and in a healthier manner.

1. You are talking to an individual who seems to be constantly
distracted. She taps her fingers, continually recrosses her legs,
glances at people walking by her office, and keeps interrupting
you to make observations of her own. She seems to be uninter-
ested in your particular problems.

2. At a meeting, the chairman allows the conversation to continue well past the point of productive debate. It seems to you
that all pertinent information was generated at least an hour
before, and that the available options are clear. Yet he allows
anyone with something to say to keep talking, even those who
only rehash things that had seemingly been agreed to earlier. It
seems as if the decision may never be made, but rather, will be
eternally debated.

3. You've prepared a lengthy and quite detailed report about ways available to implement a new performance review system. Yet your manager doesn't read it. Instead, he keeps asking you how quickly it can be installed and what might be the major obstacles to its successful acceptance. Despite the fact that you've painstakingly laid out all the contingencies in your report, he seems to want a shorthand, verbal assessment of the results he might expect. You think he's going about this by the seat of his pants.

4. You've been assigned to work on a special project with two people from Sales whom you've never met. They insist on meeting during lunch and after work over cocktails, although there is permission and time to work on the project during the workday. Moreover, they waste most of the time you spend together talking about irrelevant issues and are very interested in your background, your interests, and your attitudes. They've even suggested that the three of you go to a local sports event over the weekend. They seem convinced that the better you get to know each other, the better the project work will be. You're convinced that the only thing you're going to gain is weight.

5. A colleague has promised you that he will go to bat for you to support a critical addition to your staff that you need. In return, you've loaned him resources to complete an overdue project that his department had been having trouble with. But now you find that your colleague hasn't supported you as promised and claims that his only obligation was to give you moral support and to not oppose the addition. A third colleague complains that he's done the same to her—refusing to transfer budget funds for people she loaned him, claiming that he promised to do it only if she went over budget at the end of the year. You both are wondering what other promises he has made that he will not fulfill.

6. You have been urging one of your managers for over a month to take action on a performance problem in his area. He repeatedly assures you that he will, but you've discovered that he hasn't had even one conversation with the person whose performance is creating both productivity and morale problems for the entire division. You can't understand his reluctance. He seems to have excellent relationships with his subordinates, is extremely well-liked, and readily provides recognition and rewards for his people. Yet he clearly is procrastinating about talking to this employee. You realize that you're probably going to have to do this yourself.

7. One of your finest customer service representatives has requested and been granted a transfer into Sales. She was an outstanding performer, and the move seemed to promise the

simultaneous benefits of recognition for an outstanding employee and a much needed addition to the sales force. However, she has been a changed person in Sales. Her results are not only poor, but her call rate is far below average, despite being given high-priority prospects. She has become moody and temperamental. You're convinced that something at home must have occurred to cause this abrupt change in behavior. But you don't feel you can move her back to Customer Service without disrupting the operation, compromising your confidence in her, and hurting the promotional chances of others.

8. One of your best managers consistently fails to get reports to you on time or properly completed. Her area's results are excellent, but the reporting is a continuing annoyance to you. She promises to improve her reports and sometimes briefly does; but she inevitably falls back into her old pattern. You're considering giving her a negative performance rating as a way to "motivate" her to improve her reporting, although, in truth, you are somewhat leery of tampering with the motivation of such a good performer.

9. You're experiencing a dreadful record in the selection of personnel. Despite every precaution—including a series of interviews with carefully prepared questions—many of the new recruits simply aren't measuring up. In fact, it seems that your "hit" rate is no better than 50/50. You might as well be flipping a coin with each candidate, yet each one seems excellent in the interview and their track records are superb. You're not quite sure what mistake you're making, but you know that the competition is certainly doing better than you are at retaining new hires.

How many of these situations sound familiar? And what is the normal reaction of your colleagues and yourself? It's common to make value judgments ("He's a liar," and "He couldn't manage his way out of a phone booth") or incorrect assumptions ("There must be something bothering her off the job," and, "The change was probably too abrupt") or to take invalid actions ("Let's train new people for longer periods," and, "The compensation system is in need of improvement").

What you're actually seeing in many such cases, however, is behavioral predispositions that haven't been accommodated or aren't appropriate. In example 1, we have an impatient person who needs to hear things quickly and succinctly; the manager in example 2, on the other hand, wants to build consensus and places a premium on all facts being heard and examined. In example 3, we have a firm, risk-taking manager who doesn't want to bother reading reports. Example 4 shows highly sociable people wanting to establish a comfortable relationship as a prelude to getting down to work. The colleague in example 5 does not have much consideration for others and seems to be very low on the self-confidence scale. In example 6, the manager is so sociable and relationship-oriented that he is loath to jeopardize a relationship even though poor performance is going unaddressed. Example 7 is about the prototypical service person whose work is excellent but who is uncomfortable initiating relationships. The excellent manager in example 8 is simply very low on the attention-to-detail scale, though she performs excellently in her job. And your personnel selections in example 9 are too influenced by candidates who paint a self-portrait that works for the interview but, at least half the time, can't be sustained on the job.

These are quite real job concerns, ones you face daily at work. Our actions are perfectly explicable and understandable in behavioral terms, but our responses in circumstances like those described above are often as nonproductive as the difficult behaviors of others because our responses are based on our own ideas of what is acceptable or appropriate behavior. Managers who expect to intelligently manage people *must* understand the ramifications of behavior and make appropriate adjustments.

Niccolo Machiavelli once wrote that the successes or failures of men depended on their ability to suit their behavior to the times. This is no less true for managers than it was for princes.

General Guidelines for Managing Behavior

We'll end this chapter on applying skills by focusing on the positive. How do managers deal with success? One study has shown that people with a positive attitude *and the ability to get along with others* seldom get sick.[11] They see change—whether good or bad—as an opportunity for growth. Such people have a sense of control over their lives and are deeply committed to and interested in their work and other activities.

Success—be it a promotion, achievement, recognition, acceptance—brings with it change. It's not uncommon to hear of the "sore winner," or the person who is ruined by good fortune. Just as we should be able to take setbacks in stride, we should similarly be able to integrate life's victories into our work and social environment. There's nothing wrong with popping champagne, but you're in trouble if it creates a hangover that affects performance and subverts judgments.

Seventeen years ago, recently out of school and convinced I knew everything there was to know, I had my first article published. It was called "Selecting and Training an Assistant." Never mind that I was someone's assistant—ensconced deep in the engine room of Prudential's management structure—and that I had never selected and trained anyone. If I could publish an article on the subject, *clearly* I knew all about it. Two hundred articles, four books, and three consulting firms later, however, I've come to realize how much I *don't* know. However, this discovery is not sufficient to dampen a writer's spirit.

Similarly, in this world of upward mobility and competition for fewer organizational opportunities, we often find newly promoted managers ready and enthusiastic but insufficiently prepared for the demands of their prized new positions. They certainly have the potential for success, but they often need some help in the transition. Here, then, are some general guidelines, compiled from a series of counseling sessions I've held with fast-track people from the middle management through the executive levels.

1. *Always maintain your sense of humor.* Humor is one of the best antidotes to stress—especially when we aim it at our own foibles. It also does wonders in restoring perspective; after all, we are but an obscure footnote in the course of civilization. I've found that people who laugh easily, both at themselves and at circumstances, are more adaptable and flexible. A promotion shouldn't force you to leave your sense of humor behind. And a promotion shouldn't make you stop encouraging humor in subordinates.

2. *Support, reward, and defend your good people.* Take a tough stance on poor performers and marginal people. Many newly promoted managers seem to have a need to prove they can "save" everyone, but making tough people decisions is trial by fire for a manager.

3. *Delegate all the responsibility and authority that your ego will allow.* Being secure is *acting* secure. Managers are paid to achieve results, which require thinking much more than acting. Don't be lulled into the trap of perpetual activity and mistaking it for results. Sometimes the toughest decision a manager must make is to do nothing, to wait, and to ponder.

4. *Be selfish.* You can't help anyone else when you are weak or threatened yourself. Make sure that you have the resources, space, leeway, and clout that you need to perform well. There is nothing immoral or illegal in looking out for yourself, particularly in those areas where your well-being can directly affect others.

5. Do the unexpected. A surprise gift, trip, or other perk for a subordinate might be far more appreciated than a scheduled pay raise. This must be one of the most overlooked and underused motivational techniques available to managers. In fifteen years of working for other people in three different organizations, I can recall only one time when a superior did something like this. He said, "Here are two plane tickets for you and your wife. You both deserve them." I supported that person through thick and thin and maintain a strong relationship with him to this day. We all become so busy fighting fires that we forget to even consider doing the unexpected. Managers who don't have time to extend a lunch invitation, a public pat on the back, or a small perquisite simply don't have the time to do their jobs correctly. Managers in a Fortune 500 company recently expressed to me their outrage and indignation in behalf of a colleague who was retiring after forty-five years on the job and hadn't received a visit from a single vice president, even though several were only ten minutes away.

6. Jefferson said, *"In matters of taste, swim with the current. In matters of principle, stand like a rock."* This distinction is absolutely vital to managers ascending the corporate ladder. Assuming a bellicose stand on every issue will dilute your influence just as much as seeming indecisive on major concerns. It's important to separate ethics, values, and critical business goals from preferences, biases, and short-term desires. Oscar Wilde said, "A thing is not necessarily true because a man died for it." So, too, in business. Pick your battles, and if you put your reputation and status on the line, make sure the issues are worth "dying" for.

7. Enforce policies totally or not at all. This has nothing to do with flexibility or situational judgments. It has everything to do with respect for your position and respect for the organization. Whether it's accepting lunch from prospective vendors, flying first class, arriving on time for meetings, or dealing with customer complaints, ignoring transgressions will inevitably create disrespect for *all* policies. After all, who knows where the line will finally be drawn? Change policies you can't defend, and consistently support and enforce those you can. But if you break the rules yourself, expect the floodgates to promptly swing open.

8. Remember that the grapevine and rumor mill carry information and opinion efficiently, widely, and dramatically. Don't ignore the informal communication system. Plug into it. Let it be known that you're approachable. Develop a network of informal contacts at a variety of levels so that you can evaluate as comprehensively as possible what's really going on. Above all, if you find your direct reports agreeing with you an inordinate amount of the time and you get the feeling you're walking on water, look down. Your ankles are probably already under.

9. Strive only for excellence. At worst, you'll be consistently competent. At best, you'll consistently shine. Don't enter into any responsibility or project thinking you'll only work hard enough to "get by," or worse, being concerned only with keeping your flanks covered. In the first place, there's no magic in it, nothing to stimulate yourself or others. In the second place, the overwhelming odds are that you didn't get to where you are through excess caution. There's no reason to think you need to exercise it now.

10. In the crunch, go with your instincts. I'm a great believer in rationality and analysis of information. But there are occasions—some of them crucial—when there are no appropriate templates or systems to fall back on. Don't hesitate to go with your gut. Management is art and science, and the higher you rise, the more art begins to predominate. You can teach virtually anyone to use a decision matrix, but you can't teach judgment. In the best-run organizations I've seen, the question, "What's the *right* thing to do?" is the one top managers are constantly asking, especially in uncharted waters.

Coping with promotion is a pleasant problem when you realize that the key to success is to do consciously what you've already been doing so well.

Notes

1. "Caught in the Middle," *Business Week*, 12 September 1988, p. 80.
2. As cited in "Stressed Employees Look for Relief in Workers' Compensation Claims," *Wall Street Journal*, 7 April 1988.
3. As cited in *Changing Times* (April 1988).
4. "The Crippling Ills That Stress Can Trigger," *Business Week*, 18 April 1988, p. 77.
5. Spencer-Graham, Inc. (New York stress management consultants), "Stress in the Work Environment," as cited in *American Society for Training and Development Journal*.
6. Donald DeCarlo (counsel for the American Insurance Association), as quoted in "Stressed Employees. . . ."
7. "Stress: The Test Americans Are Failing," *Business Week*, 18 April 1988, p. 74.
8. "U.S.: Job Stress a Health Problem," *Providence Journal*, 3 October 1986.
9. As cited in "Stressed Employees. . . ."
10. Alan Weiss, "The Fine Art of Managing Stress," *Training News* (December 1983): 16.
11. Study by psychologist Suzanne Kobasa, cited in Blair Justice, *Who Gets Sick* (Houston: Peak Press, 1987).

6

Select, Don't Settle: The Most Important Decision of All

Others judge us by what we've done;
we judge ourselves by what we know
we're capable of doing.
—Longfellow

The most expensive decisions any manager makes are selection decisions. Yet managers are notoriously ill prepared and poorly equipped to perform well in this area. Every day, poor hires, promotions, transfers, and assignments are lowering productivity, undermining morale, and adversely affecting the customer.

The starting point for resolving this problem is the understanding that past performance is generally not an indicator of future success. Behavior is.

Factors Affecting Performance

There's a classic question that Bob Mager and Peter Pipe ask in *Analyzing Performance Problems:* "Could he do it if his life depended on it?"[1] If you put a gun to subordinates' heads and threatened to pull the trigger unless they perform the job, there are only two possibilities: (1) They perform and yell, "Don't shoot!" In this case, you have an attitude problem. (2) They can't perform, and you have to shoot them. Here, you have a skills problem—they'd certainly perform if they knew how.

Factors that affect ability include:

- Experience
- Aptitude

- Mental capacity
- Education/knowledge
- Physical capacity
- Comprehension

In this "can-do" area, the primary interventions are training and assistance. For example, a person who "can't do" a task might have to learn how to do it, or might only need a job aid or physical aid for help in doing it. Learning how to lock the bank vault is critical to performing that task, but so is a ladder or a taller colleague if one is not tall enough to reach the switch that primes the alarm.

These kinds of interventions are the easy part. They are helpful when trying to raise skill levels or increase knowledge. These approaches are tangible and impersonal and rely on easily obtainable information. ("Can you do this? Let me see you do it. Has anyone ever taught you the role of these?")

It's the "want-to" factors, however, that move people with ability from mediocre performance and "consent" to superior performance and "commitment." Yet, it's much more difficult to ask, "*Why* don't you do it this way?" than it is to ask, "*Can* you do this?" Many people who are asked the first question can't identify the true cause of their stress, their unwillingness to apply themselves, or their uninterest in sustaining high performance.

"Want-to" is much more nebulous than "can-do," but here are some specific factors that tend to affect motivation:

- Goal clarity
- Normative pressures
- Feedback
- Power
- Personal values
- Goal compatibility
- Incentives
- Self-interest
- Leadership
- Acceptance
- Organizational values
- Stress

These factors do not require training or job aids. They do require assessments and responses to job compatibility issues.

An individual who places great stock in being accepted by others and in having his or her expertise respected might have a profile similar to this:

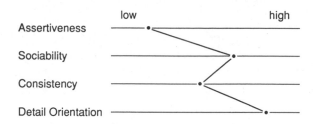

If this individual is placed in a job that requires a high level of assertiveness and leaves no time to work on being accepted, he or she will be frustrated and unhappy and no matter how skilled, no matter how knowledgeable, will not *want* to perform—or at least not to full potential. The investment simply isn't justified by the return.

Past Performance and Future Success

Take the case of the division executive who brilliantly ran division X but can't make the transition to division Z. Has the executive lost his or her skills in the transition period? Was the executive simply overrated and lucky to begin with, and now can't measure up? Is the "chemistry" not right in the new surroundings? Are the stars portending difficult times ahead?

Although these are commonly cited causes, what's usually happening is that the behaviors that stood the executive in good stead in the former position are not the behaviors necessary for success in the new position. As we explained in the last chapter, prior performance is not an indicator of future success. The appropriate behaviors for the position are the only reliable indicators of success. An executive who was forceful, authoritative, risk-taking, and impatient in one division might now find himself in a division in which success depends on consensus-building, careful analysis of facts, and conformance with established procedure. The executive may have neither the flexibility nor the range of behaviors to accommodate these new requirements. Moreover, when he begins to employ those very traits that accounted for his previous success, he is hit with charges of insensitivity, poor people skills, and "breaking the rules." These are expensive—often devastating—errors for the executive as well as the organization, yet we see them happen repeatedly in many organizations.

Once, when interviewing someone for a sales position, I came across a candidate who was outgoing, dynamic, bold—in short, the kind of person who I thought was a perfect sales recruit. He would walk into a room of people and immediately establish strong, comfortable relationships. However, after some testing and follow-up, I learned that while he was gregarious and persuasive, he actually hated to initiate sales calls! He tended to take "no" as a personal rejection. The relationship was far more important to him than the task at hand. Yet he could fool most people in an interview (or at least, he could fool me) because, to preserve the relationship, he would do everything possible to come across as the ideal candidate. He would readily demonstrate as much aggressiveness as necessary, although he could never *sustain* such behavior for very long after the interview—and certainly not for long under actual job conditions. It was as vital for him as it was for me to understand exactly what the repercussions of these behaviors would be in his future performance.

Selection as Art

On an alarmingly regular basis, organizations throw money at "training problems," "motivation problems," or "communication problems" that were created by putting the wrong person in the job. Poor selection is the first teetering domino that creates a massive crash down the line. Good selection doesn't guarantee success, but poor selection guarantees failure.

An engaging personality is *not* the help to salespeople that it's often thought to be. The ability to gain trust is more important to selling success than likability. I've worked with hundreds of salespeople who are charming and gregarious and who nurture the prospect's every wish. Their activities—and expense accounts—reflect their orientation toward building a relationship with the client. Unfortunately, many of them never got around to *asking for the business*. They didn't want to jeopardize the relationship.

Some years ago, an upscale New York City clothing retailer called Barney's used "Select, Don't Settle" as its advertising slogan. I always thought it was a wonderfully alliterative phrase, evoking the difference between controlling your destiny and being controlled by events. I'm sure it sold a lot of socks for Barney's, which remains a thriving enterprise today. But since the store no longer uses the slogan, perhaps managers engaged in selection could appropriate it.

Proper selection of people is one of the most vital and neglected skills in management's repertoire. Most managers make frequent selection decisions—hiring, promotions, transfers, assignments— yet few are taught the necessary skills to make these decisions intelligently; even fewer receive any reinforcement or feedback about how well they're using such skills. As a result, most managers don't make selection decisions at all. They simply settle for a warm body that is willing and available.

Consider your own experience as an interviewee. How often have you been interviewed, counseled, or evaluated by people who talked 90 percent of the time and listened only half-heartedly the other 10 percent? I timed one interview in which a manager spoke for fifty-two minutes out of sixty and, on the basis of what "exchange," made a hiring decision. The candidate turned down the offer.

Even though hiring decisions are critical, the process is often treated as an afterthought. Interviews are squeezed in as time permits, without so much as a vague attempt at strategy or procedure. When a candidate is required to go through a series of interviews, succeeding interviewers get little background information (which they tend not to review anyway) and have no idea of where the candidate stands in the process. Who's to blame? Everyone who knowingly participates in such chaos.

A sensible hiring process has some basic rules that all managers should be taught:

- Before meeting the candidate, the interviewer should study a clearly written job description that includes the competencies and behaviors necessary for success.

- All interviewers should follow a structured, systematic interview process to gather the information necessary to judge the candidate fairly and objectively.

- Tests or outside interviews should be used to check for consistency, missing information, and red flags.

- Subsequent interviews (more than one should be required for any serious candidate) should expand upon issues addressed in previous interviews, not merely cover the same ground in a new setting.

- Newly hired employees should be monitored to determine if the hiring decision was a good one. All employees who quit during the first year should go through an exit interview.

- The results of this monitoring should be shared with all managers who hire employees. These periodic updates should include time to reinforce selection skills and identify and resolve problems.

Many managers are unable and often unwilling to track the results of their hiring decisions over time. They remain blissfully unaware of the consequences of their decisions, often blaming training, personality conflicts, miscommunication, and other scapegoats. I opened one executive's eyes by showing her that her failure rate was 61 percent. Well over half of her hires had to be terminated within the year! She might as well have flipped a coin with every applicant. It's clearly someone's job to teach the necessary hiring skills and monitor their application, if only because the average poor selection decision at the middle management level costs an organization $40,000.[2]

Selection interviewing is not one of the sexiest items in the average course catalogue. There is no "one-minute selector" (thank goodness), and you can't "hire people by wandering around." But no set of skills is more critical for long-term productivity and performance in any enterprise.

Making the right hiring decisions can mean the difference between success and failure for a company. The challenge is to find people whose strengths you need and to put them in positions where they can use those skills and aptitudes. All companies know that to do a job, an employee must be physically capable of doing it and must have the right knowledge and skills for it. But as mentioned before, it's surprising how many firms neglect temperament—how suited the applicant is to the work.

Star athletes—people with big egos and the confidence to make the dramatic play under pressure—are usually unsuccessful as team managers. A manager needs a kind of personality stars rarely possess: patient and attentive to detail. Each game for the manager is a long chess match, where one probes the opposition's assets and weaknesses, planning responses several moves ahead.

What should employers do? Interviewing carefully before making personnel changes may help, but oddly enough, the information you need is hard to get.

Simple, well-designed behavioral tests scored by consultants or by your own company can identify the most important characteristics that come into play in business: aggressiveness, sociability, and so forth, plus other qualities like confidence, sensitivity, impulsiveness, and patience. You may prefer to have your prospect interviewed by many people from your company or by many from the outside, each exploring different ground.

Ah, you may say, but can't people be trained to modify their behavior? As we've stressed in earlier chapters, the key questions for an employer are: Modified how much? For how long? At what cost?

A field claims adjuster for an insurance company must deal with policyholders who feel they are being shortchanged, who have faced emotional traumas, police officials, and so on. Place someone in this position who likes things to be routine, and you'll see an intelligent employee conducting incomplete investigations, misadjusting claims, and burning out in exhausted confusion before much time has passed.

It's amazing how many organizations mistake this for a training problem and throw away money on sharpening skills to resolve what is really a discrepancy between job and temperament. This is akin to tuning up your car because the tires are low. Only the mechanic gains.

I don't say that behavioral testing should be mechanically applied. You have the responsibility of developing your own particular staff. For instance, hiring blackjack dealers at a casino requires screening out people whose minds are too lively; such people get bored with the monotony of turning over cards and start finding ways to pass the time (such as cuing customers on how to beat the house in return for big tips). And yet, casinos must hire at least a few of these more creative thinkers to promote to pit bosses and managers.

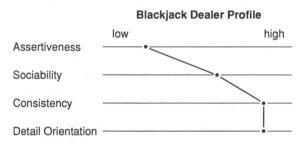

When you make your decision, your mind will be more occupied with your candidate's style, knowledge, and experience than with trying to predict his or her behavior patterns. But the more complete your information is, the better your employees' performance will conform to your hopes after you hire them.

As the proper selection, evaluation, and motivation of people become more critical, the sophistication and accuracy of an organization's methodology for accomplishing these tasks become increasingly important. Unfortunately, many of our approaches are very sophisticated about measuring the wrong thing.

Perhaps the riskiest proposition of all is using "years of experience" as a key criterion of future performance. We see this all the time: "The successful candidate will have a minimum of five years' experience." Well, the successful *candidate* might, but this may be the last qualification actually needed by the person who is capable of performing the job successfully.

One of the factors that generates years of experience is mediocrity—some people are good enough to hang on but are not good enough to do better. "You won't get rich, but you won't get fired" is the operating principle. Are these the people you want for a critical job—someone else's average performers?

In September 1984, *Management Review* ran a brief piece on "potential" appraisals as opposed to traditional performance appraisals—that is, comparing candidates to the demands of the future position and deemphasizing their performance in past positions.[3] One might consider it an approach geared toward conditions that inevitably change, rather than toward static conditions. Although it describes only one company's work in this area (Ebasco Services, Inc.), this article was one of the few of the period to focus on a topic of major concern for the 1990s: how do you measure and evaluate the capacity for future performance?

Change has become the norm, not the exception. When you consider the dramatic changes occurring within businesses such as banking, publishing, insurance, and communications, and the rapidity with which job descriptions must change to keep pace, it should become alarmingly clear why *potential* performance is the proper selection criterion.

Take even the bank that has become superb at selecting, training, and developing loan officers, for example. It still faces a whole new ballgame because the roles and performances required of that position are radically changing. The mortgage officer who once sat in an office seeing applicants on a scheduled basis in a sellers' market must now, in a competitive market, pursue people at home, at work, in the evening, and on weekends. Can the individual chosen for the old job perform equally well in the new one? More importantly, should the bank still be looking at all for the old kind of employee?

The traditional American aspiration has been toward constant vertical mobility. Work hard, establish a lifestyle, get promoted, work hard, establish a better lifestyle. . .But now the aspiration and the reality are changing dramatically. The advent of the two-income family is less a result of female equality than of the threat that this generation would not lead a lifestyle equal to or better than that of the previous one. We're also seeing a reduction in the number of rungs on the corporate ladder. The decreasing number of positions in middle management, the maturation of the baby boomers, and a record number of MBA graduates have produced more people pursuing fewer openings.

While this situation is ideal for the organization seeking to select only the cream of the crop for key jobs, it also places more strain than ever on the apparatus for selecting the right person. At worst, political expediency or seniority alone decides. But even at best, past performance is all too often the key criterion.

Selection based on behavioral factors is no black art, no crystal ball endeavor. Rather, it is a professional, systematic, and forward-thinking approach that should be *the* major determinant in selection decisions of all kinds.

Selection as Science

The only sane conclusion that one can make after observing organizational hiring practices is that people prefer to hire incompetents. (Peter Drucker: "Experience has shown that the only thing in abundant supply is the universal incompetent.")[4] Why is this? Well, incompetents certainly make the boss look better. Then again, perhaps the boss is incompetent and is merely hiring in his own image. Incompetents can also take the fall if something goes wrong ("How can I be expected to accomplish anything when I'm given people like these?").

Key managers who should know better are unconsciously (one hopes) hiring incompetents into their organizations each day. This is like making certain that the termites are in the basement, the air is damp, the heat is turned up, and the pest control guy is out of town. Here are ten suggestions that will help you keep your hiring practices focused on keeping the basement dry and pest-free. Remember, no amount of training, orientation, reward, support, or any other alchemy is going to turn a poor selection into a star performer.[5]

1. Determine who will do your interviewing and train them in the art and science of personnel selection. The ultimate interviewing responsibility is the line manager's with the human resource function serving as the initial screen. These two areas should be working with a common set of objectives and job descriptions. Provide regular refreshers and simulations so that interviewing skills keep up with changing times and changing organizational needs.

2. Concentrate on general knowledge and abilities. It's easier to look for technical expertise and credentials, but this will sidetrack the process. An overemphasis on technical ability, credentials, and references tends to create a bureaucracy. But paying attention to comprehensive business knowledge, the application of that knowledge (which we can call wisdom), and the ability to relate to people creates a dynamic, flexible, *human* organization.

3. Evaluate your managers on their hiring performance.[6] Track the process, compare the results against turnover and performance, and determine who your best interviewers are. Constantly train—or remove from the process—the poorer ones, and focus the best ones on key hires. Would you deliberately send your poorest salesperson to try to sell your largest prospect? You know who your best and worst salespeople are, and you should know no less about your interviewers.

4. Almost always, ignore references. Employers aren't checking references for 75 percent of all candidates because previous employers aren't *giving* them, owing to fear of lawsuits.[7] You are probably well advised to check dates and places of employment for accuracy, but litigation has effectively nullified the possibility of obtaining useful feedback from past employers. You'll get either platitudes or no information at all, and you'll never get any negatives.

5. Shut up and listen. Not only can you learn very little about someone when you're talking about yourself and your firm, but you also give the candidate valuable hints as to how to respond when you finally do allow him or her to talk. Volunteer little, especially early on. Challenge the candidate's responses, to see what his or her reaction is to confrontation. But keep in mind that you're not trying to pass muster here, the candidate is.

6. Take all of your "dress for success" literature and give it to the Salvation Army. Of *course* you're not going to hire someone who shows up at an interview wearing a halter top or sneakers. But does it *really* tell you something if his suit is neither blue nor gray, or if she's a "winter" dressed as a "summer," or if his hair is not quite on the conservative side? Let's stop worrying about appearances, which are manipulable, and start focusing on competence, which is genuine.

7. Understand that hiring is a tough process. No one ever said it's supposed to be easy. "Get me someone within two weeks," and, "Get me the best you can find, no matter how long it takes," are instructions that will generate considerably different candidates. The higher up the hierarchy your opening, the more probable it is that you're looking for someone who is happily employed and whose resume is *not* floating all over the organization. Generally, if your own devices—advertising, contacts, networking, internal postings, and so on—have not turned up the right candidate in six weeks, you are probably best served by a professional recruiter.

8. Establish multiple interviews, but not repetitive ones. Have several interviewers see the candidate in different circumstances (office, lunch, early, late), and make certain that each successive interview picks up where the last left off. In other words, vague areas and questions from earlier interviews should be cleared up in succeeding ones. I was once interviewed by five successive people who each asked me, "What do you think you can bring to our firm?" By the third interview, after feedback from the first two, I had a smooth response, and by the fifth I was told, "Your perception is superb—those are the abilities the executive committee just discussed last week. It's like you were in the room with us."

The Interview Control Sheet provides a structure for multiple interviews that can help keep repeated questions to a minimum.

9. Get feedback from candidates. After each interview, and irrespective of whether you will recommend them, ask candidates what they thought about the session. Was the time too brief? Did they feel uncomfortable? Were their questions answered? What could have been done better? You'll learn not only how to improve sessions but still more about the candidate's honesty and composure.

10. Finally, do use psychological evaluations and/or testing by reputable sources.[8] While these shouldn't constitute the basis for your decision, they do provide more information—especially in the behavioral area—that otherwise might be unavailable. Every time you hire, you are making a huge organizational investment. Any tool available to protect that investment should be applied.

A few final words about the efficacies of testing. Most firms now require preemployment tests.[9] The Bureau of National Affairs reports that all of the companies it surveyed administer one kind of test or another to applicants for some jobs. Fully 63 percent test skills, but only 3 percent ask for tests of *competencies*. More than half give physicals, 25 percent check for drug abuse, and one percent check for AIDS. But only 7 percent were testing for honesty!

Behaviors and Professions

Let's examine basic behavioral factors in terms of professions. Choose a job that would typically require behavior ranking on

INTERVIEW CONTROL SHEET

Candidate's name: Home phone:

Home address:

Business address:

Business phone: Permission to call at work: Yes___No___

Source of contact:

Position to be filled:

Brief summary of job:

Backup attached: Job description___Behavioral profile of job*___Resume___Other___

Prior interview: Date_____Conducted by_____

Items for follow-up from prior interview:

Summary of this interview:

Next step recommended:

Further items for next interview:

Conducted by (signed)_____Date_____

*This could be in the form of the profile we've suggested, with supporting
commentary on assertiveness, sociability, consistency, detail orientation,
self-confidence, and so on.

the high and low ends of each factor below. For example, a member of the clergy should have a high consistency level to be effective, and a military officer should be highly assertive. Choose one example for each end of each factor from your own profession or from any in the public and private sector.

low		high
	Assertiveness	(military officer)
	Sociability	
	Consistency	(clergy)
	Detail Orientation	

Compare your responses with those below. Did you find that it was easier to arrive at the high-end examples than the low-end ones? Or did you tend to place "menial" jobs at the low end—janitor and secretary—and "exalted" jobs at the high—CEOs and professionals? These are common errors.

low		high
Customer relations	Assertiveness	Homicide detective
CPA	Sociability	Auto salesperson
Architect	Consistency	Public relations
CEO	Detail Orientation	Draftsperson

Note that even within professions, we need to make distinctions. For example, a traffic cop or homicide detective should be highly assertive, but that's not necessarily the behavior we want in a hostage negotiator. Imagine that approach: "We don't care who you've got in there—come out or we'll blow the place up!"

Here's a highly assertive defense attorney: "Ladies and gentlemen of the jury, I'm sure that once you see the ridiculous and shabby case that the prosecutor has feebly assembled, you'll find you have no choice but to find my client innocent of all charges. There is simply no other logical conclusion to be reached."

Now, here's an unassertive, but equally persuasive, defense attorney: "Ladies and gentlemen of the jury, I'm just an average local citizen like yourselves, and I can't match the sophistication and firepower over there at the prosecutor's table. But I am relying on you to view the evidence we've produced with objectivity, intelligence, and compassion. And I think, as reasonable people, you'll agree with our contention that my client, the widow Brown, is innocent of all charges." (Remember Jimmy Stewart in the movie *Anatomy of a Murder?*)

The people we are most comfortable approaching are usually low in assertiveness and high in the other three factors, particularly consistency. Charismatic leaders are generally both highly assertive and very sociable, though there are always clear exceptions—Gandhi easily comes to mind. But it is the Churchills, Roosevelts, and Golda Meirs who prove the rule.

Let's look at something much more personal and potentially useful. On the chart below, place a dot on each line to indicate the behavior you would consider ideal in a beginning accountant. For example, would a good accountant be fairly assertive, or not? Very low detail-oriented, or not?

```
                          low                    high

Assertiveness       ─────────────────────────────────

Sociability         ─────────────────────────────────

Consistency         ─────────────────────────────────

Detail Orientation  ─────────────────────────────────
```

We can probably agree on this profile; does yours look something like this?

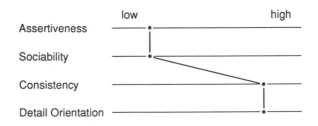

The best accountant would be fairly low-assertive and low-sociable, but fairly high in consistency and detail orientation. After all, an accountant is an individual contributor who performs similar functions repeatedly and who is rewarded for accuracy and thoroughness. While you may not have chosen the extremes, you probably agree with the general direction of this profile.

Now let's promote our accountant to manager of the financial reporting unit. With these new responsibilities, the direction of the desirable behaviors should look something like this:

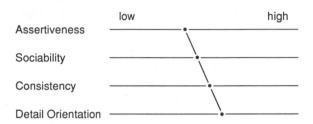

Our new manager should be somewhat more assertive and sociable, more accepting of change (less consistent), and more focused on the big picture than on the details.

Now our fast thinker becomes vice president of finance:

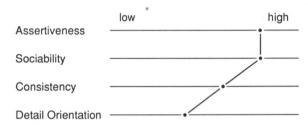

Finally, we'll promote our eager beaver to chief financial officer, a job with a profile something like this:

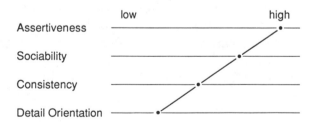

As we progress up the career track, these kinds of adjustments are not at all uncommon. Yet *very few of us possess the wide range of behaviors and the ability to change that such job progression demands.* This is why we sometimes read of people like the Merrill Lynch broker who finally made partner and then promptly left to open a bicycle shop in New Hampshire. The job, perquisites, prestige, and fringes were exactly as expected. But the behavior required in the new job was too great a stretch, and the result was either breakdown or breakout. Not everyone who should gets out.

We've exaggerated the changes in our ambitious CPA's career path, but they're not unrealistic. As you read this, organizations all over the country are promoting their best salespeople to sales management; often losing a superb salesperson and creating a lousy manager. How many such moves can an organization make and still maintain a competitive edge?

A top salesperson in most businesses has a profile something like this:

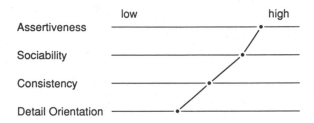

A top salesperson is assertive and sociable (slightly more assertive than sociable so as not to be afraid to ask for the sale, even if it means jeopardizing the relationship), thrives on change, and hates detail—try to get a good salesperson to turn in expense reports or sales forecasts on time and according to the instructions. What happens when the top salesperson becomes the sales manager?

This person is now more confined, must temper his or her assertiveness, and must be much more consistent and detail-oriented to follow up on exactly those issues procrastinated about in the previous job! This transformation, unlike a butterfly's metamorphosis, is not a natural act. It is often highly unnatural and causes stress and poor performance. Great salespeople do not necessarily make great sales managers. They might, but you can't assume they will.

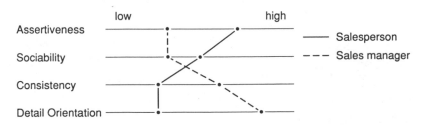

This doesn't mean that people who are good at their current jobs should never be promoted. It does mean that (a) people need preparation for promotion and assistance once promoted, based on how well their natural predispositions fit the new job, and (b) greater use should be made of alternative means of reward and recognition for people who perform well but who should be allowed to continue performing well in their current job.

IBM, for example, has created the positions of fellow, senior fellow, and executive fellow to correspond to manager, general manager, and vice president. In this way, a researcher can be promoted and can achieve higher levels of organizational recognition and reward without being removed from the basic research that created his or her success. Formerly, the only way to provide such a reward was to place the researcher into a management position. Organizations as diverse as newspapers and banks have followed IBM's lead.

There are other, less radical adjustments that can be made by both the individual and the organization to enhance behavioral fit. For instance, if your new job calls for a level of detail orientation that you don't have and aren't likely to develop an assistant can be assigned many of the detailed chores. Sometimes just having it pointed out that you need to adopt a more assertive (or consistent, or detailed, or whatever) posture for for the duration of a meeting or a given task is sufficient to help you make the adjustment.

Ten Key Competencies

But managers cannot be expected to make *all* the adjustments necessary to maintain the skills, knowledge, and behaviors—in other words, the *competencies*—that all employees must have if their organizations are to compete in tomorrow's marketplace and, one hopes, to excel. Here are ten general competencies that organizations must maintain and develop among its employees:

1. Responsibility: Employees must professionally deliver the products and services expected of them. Every employee represents the company, and every customer interaction is important, be it a returned call, mailed order, repaired product, or a smile and a "thank you."

2. Follow-through: Do what you say will do. Fulfill obligations. Monitor the operation to see if goals are being met. Reinforce those that are, improve those that are not.

3. *Respect:* Respect the customer. Don't underestimate the customer's intelligence or expectations. Ask the customer for feedback.

4. *Accessibility:* Be accessible. Don't hide behind answering services, secretaries, and bureaucracy. You are there to perform, not evade. Anyone can run from uncomfortable decisions and pressure situations. Good managers resolve such situations, and superb managers prevent most of them.

5. *Responsiveness:* Be responsive. Listen to your subordinates, customers, suppliers, agents, and any others who are on the front line. If you don't receive any feedback—or get only positive feedback—actively solicit the negatives, as well as ideas for improvements.

6. *Results orientation:* Focus on results, not activities. There's an old Chinese proverb, "It makes no sense to go to bed early to save candles if the result is twins." Bureaucracy is the subordination of ends to means.

7. *Accountability:* Make business decisions. Managers are paid to make such decisions, while lawyers, accountants, and consultants are paid to provide advice. If the lawyers, accountants, and consultants are making the decisions that direct the business, then the managers aren't necessary. The business will also stagnate because its operation is no art and all science.

8. *Awareness:* Watch the environment. What is happening, no matter how remote, that might affect you? Airline hijacking created a tremendous market for X-ray and metal detecting technology, as well as for guard services. Create and maintain sensitive contacts with the business climate around you.

9. *Innovation:* Be innovative. Problem solving is important, but it only makes you as good as you used to be. Don't be satisfied merely fixing things—seek to improve them. Fred Smith didn't try to improve the postal service—he founded Federal Express and spawned a new industry.

10. *People orientation:* Remember at all times that virtually every business is a people business. The first priority must be the proper selection, development, motivation, and rewarding of people.

Poor managemnt—which is a factor in everything from small business failures to the demise of large organizations—is the largest single cause of poor performance. In these times of turbulent change, factors such as demographic shifts, new technologies, changing lifestyles, and international competition have taken our attention away from management failings, and that's bad. We need more light and more heat on this issue. Management deserves to be on the hot seat.

Notes

1. Bob Mager and Peter Pipe, *Analyzing Performance Problems, or, You Really Oughta Wanna* (Belmont, CA: Pitman Learning, 1984), p. 30.
2. Alan Weiss, "Evaluating Candidates: Past vs. Potential," *Training News* (December 1984): 7.
3. Ibid.
4. Peter Drucker, *The Effective Executive* (New York: Harper & Row, 1966).
5. See *Wareham's Basic Business Types: Sorting Winners and Losers and Managing People for Profit* (New York: Atheneum, 1987) for a light-hearted look at poor hiring techniques.
6. See "Organizationally Reinforce Professionalism in Selection," *Training and Development Journal* (September 1987).
7. Study by Challenger, Gray & Christmas Consultants, as cited *Bottom Line*, 30 September 1988.
8. See John Byrne, "This Test May Tell You to Switch Careers," *Business Week*, 21 September 1987; Jolie Solomon "Career-Change Services Spread, Offering Advice on Where and How to Job Hunt," *Wall Street Journal*, May 1986; and Kevin Shyne, "Personality Tests Get Down to Business," *Success* (August 1984).
9. "Pre-employment Tests: More Firms Require Them," *Wall Street Journal*, 5 July 1988.

7

High Performers and High-Performance Organizations

A couple of years ago, I was unlucky enough to be chosen by the IRS for a random audit, the type in which every single item on a return is examined. I showed up at my accountant's office prepared for a draconian inquisitor and was totally disarmed by an articulate, well-dressed, 28-year-old woman with a wonderful sense of humor who began the proceedings by deadpanning, "I'm from the IRS and I'm here to help you."

The audit was completed in six hours—she canceled the entire second day as unnecessary—and I owed an additional $500 due to a legitimate error on the part of my accountant. I wasn't sure whether to laugh or cry—there was something terribly wrong with my view of the world.

More recently, on a tax return for which I was owed a refund, a woman at the end of a toll-free number took fifteen minutes to track the adventures of my refund and provided me with its current status. She then gave me her *name*, for goodness' sake, and encouraged me to contact her again. I felt quite dizzy.

What's going on here? If you can't count on the IRS to be evil, surly, and uncaring, what *is* sacred? Will the telephone company begin making repair calls at promised times? Will department stores provide courteous sales help?

Both the auditor and the taxpayer serviceperson had been vested with trust—that is, the necessary authority and techniques to be responsive to their customers' needs. The field auditor had the discretion and authority to accept certain claims on faith (thank heavens), to determine what kinds of proof she would demand, and even to reduce the items examined if things appeared early on to be in order. She told me later that she had access to two levels of supervision; each supervisor gave her feedback if she required it on how she conducted each audit. She enjoyed setting up her own schedule of travel within her territory, thought her advancement potential was excellent, and especially enjoyed the job security and the educational reimbursement.

The taxpayer serviceperson knew how to use her computer to explore the system and was encouraged to take her time with callers and to be responsible—she volunteered her name and urged me to call back if I needed more help.

When employees are trusted and made responsible, they tend to perform better because they've been given power. There is a great myth, established by some sage and perpetuated by countless believers through the ages, that "power corrupts." I prefer George Bernard Shaw: "Power does not corrupt men; fools, however, if they get into a position of power, corrupt power."

Power doesn't corrupt. *Powerlessness* corrupts. Those who lack power in an organization—those who haven't been trusted, who haven't been made responsible—create artificial power. Artificial power is generally known as bureaucracy. Bureaucracies are structures that subordinate ends to means, focus on activity rather than results, and view issues through microscopes instead of telescopes. Bureaucracies are assemblages of people creating artificial power. ("Sorry, your request must be resubmitted on the correct form," or, "You can't speak to anyone in Customer Service, you must write.") People cannot tolerate being powerless, and it's powerlessness that corrupts.

As I look around organizations, I find that those who provide their people with real power (the ability to make decisions that affect the quality of their work) tend to be less bureaucratic, while those favoring powerlessness tend to be more so.

Many organizations are in transition today, some of them having learned that bureaucracies function poorly and suffer greatly in a competitive marketplace. Decision-making power must flow downward in competitive organizations, enabling people to make decisions at virtually all levels and positions. Even the telephone company, that traditional, impersonal monolith, now finds itself (or its postdivestiture pieces) in a competitive marketplace. Recently, to my utter astonishment, I was able to get phones installed in a new office on time, even in the aftermath of a hurricane. The installer provided this simple but eloquent reason: "We're instructed to make business moves our absolute top priority because we want you to choose us as your long-distance carrier when the time comes."

Not everyone—and especially not those who are too accustomed to working in a bureaucratic environment—will be able to handle true power. Which is all the more reason to try to ensure that individual behaviors are compatible with job requirements.

Power vs. Powerlessness

Activity	Powerless	Empowered
Decision making	Can only recommend	Can implement
Evaluating subordinates	Must clear with boss	Conducts on own volition
Reacting to crises	Freezes	Acts
Risk-taking	Protects self at all costs	Operates with freedom to fail
Innovation	Fixes what's broken	Establishes new standards
Planning	Projects today's picture	Creates a future vision
Reacting to setbacks	Blames the system	Finds ways to overcome
Interpersonal relations	"Win/lose" attitude	"Win/win" attitude
Motivating others	Uses coercion	Appeals to self-interest
Hiring	Chooses likable people	Chooses competent people
Delegating	Retains control	Delegates authority with responsibility
Motivating self	"What's in it for me?"	"What's in it for us?"

Significant attention has been paid over the past several years to "empowering" employees. Providing employees with *real* decision-making authority and tangible support for their judgments is a substantive way to enhance their recognition of their power within the organization. In fact, one of the most effective ways to help subordinates change their behavior is to give them such power. Irrespective of whether they are highly asser-tive, highly consistent, ambivalent about details, and/or socially retiring, empowerment will enhance their motivation to reach their job goals.

There are many methods to achieve such sharing of power. Some of the best we've seen include:

1. *Using a participatory approach whenever possible:* There are two ways to do this: either surrender the decision-making prerogative to the group—giving everyone the power to influence the deci-sion as a peer member of the group—or make it clear that you are retaining the final decision power, but will not exercise it until after you have heard from everyone in an open forum. A funda-mental breakdown often occurs when managers let employees believe they're acting in the former mode but they're actually in the latter. Participatory decisions should be consequential ones. Allowing the group to decide where to put the soda machine or how to decorate the office will empower no one.

2. *Delegating authority with responsibility, which should be made clear, overt, and measurable:* If you've asked someone to be respon-sible for checking the quality of vendor shipments, that individual should be able to accept and reject deliveries, know your sup-port is always available, and have clear instructions specifying when higher authority is needed, when to communicate directly with the vendor, and so on. Those organizations with the best customer service operations are those that allow the telephone representative to accept exchanges, correct bills, and provide the names of others who might be helpful to the customer.

3. *Ensuring that people are responsible for implementation:* This is not the same as saying, "You've got a complaint?! Okay, you're now chairperson of the committee to take care of it." People achieve a sense of power and influence by controlling their destinies. Although there are some who prefer to be "idea people" only, most of us receive gratification from seeing our ideas through to fruition. Allow people the opportunity not just to think, but to *do.* Provide the latitude to access resources, draw up plans, and manage implementation. If you tell someone something, they might be able to repeat what you said; if you show them something, they might be able to copy what you did; but if you make them *do* something and give them feedback on their per-formance, they'll be able to repeat the skill any time they need it in the future.

Empowering people is just the first step. The second is ensur-ing that the organization is receptive to such empowerment. That's often easier said than done.

Supportive, Not Subversive, Systems

One of my clients tells the following story. A manager in a large insurance company received a check from a customer. The manager mailed the check, as per policy, to the treasury division on another floor. Two days later, the check was returned to her attached to the envelope in which it was sent, with this note attached: "You have used an R135-1 envelope to mail a check to the treasury division. This can result in a lost check. The approved envelope is R141-3. Please resubmit the item in the approved fashion."

This is a true story—who could have made it up?—and we can probably all remember others like it. Most people's reaction to receiving such a note would be something like, "Well, that's politics," or "It's the system," or "It's the bureaucracy." While such rationalizations are often used to cover up a host of inadequacies, from personal shortcomings to organizational blundering, it's nonetheless true that our systems often smite our best plans, subvert our grandest schemes, and destroy our closest collaborations. "We shape our houses, and then they shape us," said Winston Churchill. He was referring to Parliament, but the point applies to our organizational houses as well. Systems are of our own making. So why do we create and tolerate subversive ones?

To a great extent, we create intricate systems because we don't trust each other. We feel the need to protect ourselves from our comrades, so we make policies, procedures, and rules that will legislate and sanction this protection. A mechanism is then required to establish, convey, and enforce the policies. This is the breeding ground for the "system for its own sake," which I define as:

1. People and resources that should be utilized in the basic business of the organization being diverted from that more profitable role; and

2. An overabundance of people and resources that are unnecessary to the basic business of the organization and are a drain on profitability.

Subversive systems hurt us all in far more insidious ways than simply encumbering our efforts to get our jobs done. They eat into our paychecks and stockholder equity and inhibit the organization's ability to grow. Of course, any organization, be it a factory, airline, city administration, or seminary, needs rules in order to operate efficiently. But the degree to which rules are formalized and enforced is a matter of flexibility, to say the least.

Trust is a Two-Way Street

Employees in any organization must be able to trust two sets of people: their leadership, and each other. Managers can readily exhibit trust by providing employees with the unfettered authority, responsibility, and resources to independently meet job goals. If such trust is present, then short-term inequities can and usually will be accepted and tolerated in the belief that they will be corrected in the longer term. And *every* organization inevitably has inequities over the short term—involving compensation, perquisites, dress codes, assignments, and so forth—especially those organizations in competitive, dynamic, or rapidly growing fields.

In organizations where trust is poor, short-term inequities are generally dealt with by the individual in one of two ways:

First, each perceived inequity becomes its own battleground. Consequently, every manager is forced to defend every decision involving people and eventually becomes conservative and gun-shy. Anyone receiving special treatment from a manager becomes fair game for *ad hominem* attack, regardless of his or her merit. Thus, an act intended to reward one person usually results in making several people unhappy. Everyone seeks "equity," a word as debased as Confederate money. And equity in this context only sets the stage for mediocrity.

The second tactic is to store up the perceived inequities until an explosion finally vents the trapped heat—almost invariably at performance review time. Past inequities tend to color every negotiation and dialogue, with emotion replacing logic. "It's time for me to get mine!" becomes the rallying cry.

Just as an organization can't be managed through its compensation system (which only perpetuates existing inequities and creates new ones), it also shouldn't be managed through a bureaucracy, or a "system." Superb, performance-oriented management requires trust. Nothing hinders an organization's growth, slows its operations, or dampens its spirit as well and as thoroughly as a lack of trust.

Peter Drucker has observed that laws passed in reaction to a wrongdoing are inevitably bad laws.[1] They're based on emotion, not reason, and they punish ninety-nine innocents in order to foil one miscreant. The same observation applies, I believe, to organizations and their rules. We all face cold, sluggish bureaucracies daily: we register our cars, we apply for loans, we try to correct phone bills. We can avoid creating monolithic bureaucracies in our workplaces, however, if we trust our leaders and our colleagues. People and organizations can grow in concert.

Self-Actualizing Organizations = High-Performance Organizations

Abraham Maslow's famous "hierarchy of needs" has served for decades as a model of how our priorities evolve as successive goals are met. Beginning with the need for security and safety, and proceeding through recognition and status, the hierarchy terminates in "self-actualization," the ability to realize one's full potential. The individual who labors through a grumbling day in an unpleasant job, only to return to a disagreeable family and dream of what might have been, is several yards short of self-actualization. However, people running their own businesses that exploit their personal talents and interests, whether it's Federal Express or the local photography shop, and whose personal lives complement and support their professional pursuits, probably have a significant sense of fulfillment.

Organizations are not substantially different. Some seem to be constantly struggling for survival, others are seeking recognition, while a chosen few are realizing their full potential. (At this writing, Eastern Airlines is on the survival level, MCI on the recognition level, and Merck & Co. on the self-actualization level.) In *The Effective Executive*, Drucker notes, "An organization is not, like an animal, an end in itself, and successful by the mere act of perpetuating the species. An organization is an organ of society, and fulfills itself by the contribution it makes to the outside environment[2] (and, presumably, by the contribution the environment makes to it).

The more employees find self-fulfillment in their work, the more likely it is that the organization can fulfill itself (reach its business goals and contribute to the environment), not merely "perpetuate the species." In fact, organizational and individual performance are more interrelated today than ever before. It's increasingly improbable that an organization can reach the top of its industry by mindlessly exploiting its work force, and it's equally unlikely that even superb management can do much with inadequate human resources. "Content expertise—simply knowing what the business does—is no longer sufficient for management. Every business is a people business today, and every manager must become adept at managing employees' performance. Human behavior is the essential component in that management.

Here are five questions to help you assess how well you and your organization manage performance.

1. Do we know that we have the right people, and that their values are compatible with and supportive of the organization's goals?

2. Have we structured our positions so that people are able to perform in the way we desire?

3. Have we communicated our expectations accurately and provided sufficient recognition and reward so that people can routinely achieve these goals?

4. Have we provided training in the people management skills required to accomplish these goals?

5. Are my management team and I setting the proper example for achievement of our performance goals?

Such human resource planning, however, is not a common organizational discipline. Only 21 percent of organizations surveyed by Hay Consultants reported having a formal system, and another 30 percent called their efforts "rudimentary or undeveloped."[3]

The key steps to creating an internal system that accommodates personal and organizational growth are assessing where you currently are and establishing the feedback mechanisms you'll need to monitor progress along the way. The first is relatively simple; the second is often extraordinarily difficult. ("Few men are wise enough to prefer useful criticism to treacherous praise," said Le Duc de la Rochefoucauld.)

The Corporate/Individual Equation

Organizational performance is affected by many factors; the standard ones are described below.

INFLUENCES ON ORGANIZATION PERFORMANCE

Strategic Factors
(technology, method of sale,
production capabilities,
services offered, etc.)

Human Resource Performance
(physical abilities, skills and
knowledge, behaviors)

Outside Environment
(competition, regulation,
economy, society, etc.)

Organization Performance
(attainment of quality, volume, return, share,
deadlines, yield, image, etc.)

Inside Environment
(policies, leadership,
culture, relationships, etc.)

Financial Resources
(credit, interest,
diversity, etc.)

Of this combination of factors, the human resource performance is the most critical to organizational performance *because it affects all other contributing factors as well.* The policies and culture established, the access to and management of finances, the anticipation of and reaction to outside influences, and the formulation of strategy are largely dependent on the competence of the people engaged in these activities.

An equation for individual performance might look something like this:

$$\text{Job Performance} = \text{Motivation} \times \text{Ability (Behavior + Skills and Knowledge)},$$

where

Job Performance = the achievement of goals required if the job is to make its contribution to organizational success and performance,

Motivation = the sustained desire to achieve goals—the "want-to-do" aspect, and

Ability = the capacity to apply the requisite skills and knowledge to achieve goals—the "can-do" aspect.

In this equation, ability represents both physical capabilities and mental skills, and knowledge and motivation represent the compatibility of individual behaviors with job requirements needed to provide sustained performance (and eventually, one hopes, self-actualization).

There are only four possible combinations of motivation and ability. People may have neither the ability nor the motivation for the job. Or they may have a high degree of each. Or, and quite commonly, they may possess a surfeit of one and a dearth of the other. Therefore, we may plot performance in this manner:

MOTIVATION/ABILITY RELATIONSHIPS

Ability		
High	Mixed Performance 4	High Performance 1
	Low Performance 3	Mixed Performance 2
Low		High
	Motivation	

In quadrant 1, we find the individual with the skills and ability to do the job ("can-do") and the behavioral fit that provides the motivation to sustain high performance ("want-to-do"). In quadrant 3, we have the usually obvious case of low or nonperformance by someone with neither the skills nor the willingness to do the job.

But it's quadrants 2 and 4 that cause the most serious problems for organizational performance—because they represent those who often appear to be *high* performers. Consequently, managers and organizations often tolerate erratic performers in the belief that these individuals are performing as well as possible.

In quadrant 2, we find someone whose behaviors are appropriate and who *wants* to do a quality job, but whose skills are not sufficient to produce top performance. This person plugs away, but constantly stumbles. This is the person who's often accused of "working hard but not working smart." Eventually, this person will become frustrated from working too hard to compensate for inadequate skills and knowledge, motivation will erode, and he or she will slide into quadrant 3.

In quadrant 4, we find the converse. This is the person who has all the ability in the world but isn't motivated to excel. He or she *can* do the job, but doesn't *want* to do it. This is the individual who takes shortcuts, uses the least effort to achieve the minimum performance that will satisfy management, and works "smart" but never hard. This is the superb athlete who plays a good offense (easily visible) but loafs on defense (often invisible). This individual causes substantial productivity loss.

The usefulness of such a breakdown—and note that we've applied no labels—is in recognizing each of these different relationships needs to be addressed differently. Throwing training dollars at the low motivation problem is as wasteful as trying to improve the attitude of the employee with the poor skills problem.

Corporate Culture and Values

Corporate "culture" has suffered from the same kind of linguistic debasement that has affected words like "strategy" or "communications." ("We need a sales strategy." "What's our strategy for this meeting?" "Is this part of our operating strategy?" "We need to strategize a response to this letter.") So let's begin with a simple, concise definition:

> Corporate culture comprises the values, beliefs, and behaviors that represent the core identity of an organization.

The McDonald's culture values absolutely uniform products and services delivered in a prescribed fashion. In the 3M culture, researchers are encouraged to "go against the grain" and know they have the freedom to fail. In the Mercedes culture, state-of-the-art engineering is emphasized regardless of cost. And at Singapore Airlines, the culture focuses on delivering unexcelled levels of passenger service.

A strong culture is imperative if an organization is to help employees fulfill themselves on the job. A strong culture will help guide behavior, particularly when there's no policy, precedent, or procedure to provide guidance. Otherwise, informal—and often debilitating—social pressures may prevail. There's a big difference between asking, "How can I protect myself?" when an unusual and vociferous customer complaint is lodged and asking, "What's the best for our customer?" The presence of a strong, positive culture will tend to generate the second question. A negative culture will produce the first.

This core identity helps establish ground rules that will influence behavior and establish appropriate expectations. It will provide a sense of purpose for employees and reduce ambiguity about objectives (one of the two primary sources of conflict discussed in Chapter 5). Ambiguity and uncertainty are especially difficult for people to deal with in trying to make daily decisions about their jobs and performance expectations.

Organizations with these characteristics generally have strong cultures:

1. *The organization stands for something that's clear and explicit.* Virtually every employee could easily articulate it. At Federal Express, everyone knows that the package "absolutely, positively, must get there the next day." It's simple to make decisions and to gear performance to that vivid goal.

2. *The corporate values are shared by all employees at all levels.* No one is "beneath" or "beyond" the corporate values. Frito-Lay is famous for its route drivers who will bend over backwards to satisfy even a minor request from a tiny store miles off the beaten track.

3. *Top management actively shapes the values so that they correspond to the business environment.* Values are organic and dynamic and reflect changing conditions and circumstances. Postdivestiture AT&T had a difficult time changing its values to those of a competitive, market-oriented organization. Lee Iacocca shifted Chrysler's values from "let's copy the competition" to "let's provide the finest," with dramatic results in the marketplace.

4. *Top management devotes time and energy to exemplifying the values for all the organization to see.* General Motors management espoused the philosophy, "These are tough times for all of us," but created serious problems for itself when it handed out large executive bonuses during a time of employee cutbacks. The CEO of Johnson & Johnson, on the other hand, in his corporation's tradition of valuing the public's trust in its products, personally faced the press and assured the public during the Tylenol tampering crisis.

5. *Employee involvement is encouraged at every level.* The Japanese are noted for their comprehensive approaches in this area: massive suggestion systems, quality circles, employee improvement teams, and frequent discussions with customers. "Management by wandering around" does no one any good unless questions are asked and people are heard during the wandering.

There are, of course, inherent risks in trying to create a corporate culture that supports business goals. These risks are sometimes overlooked by those engaged in "culture change" and "organizational transformation." The most important pitfalls are:

1. *Lip service support from senior management:* I still remember the senior vice president whose response to people refusing to participate in one of his "voluntary" productivity programs was, "Well, what can we expect? These people are the dregs of the company, that's why they're given to me in Customer Service!" His every action exemplified the opposite of what his stated goals were: he arrived late and left early, took long lunches in a separate executive dining room, was unapproachable except through his direct reports, and openly criticized his peers. Policy statements and fancy slogans are insufficient. Only action from the top will mean anything to middle management.

2. *Inconsistency:* One of my utility clients emphasized strict adherence to policies and procedures, yet its executives made frequent exceptions for large customers—very visible exceptions, since the officers had to inform front-line supervision of the special treatment requested. Lack of respect for one value will erode respect for all values.

3. *Continuing to make win/lose evaluations:* This means that for someone to win, someone else must lose, be it colleague, customer, vendor, or another department. Most attempts at culture change will be subverted unless employees are given the latitude to make mistakes and learn from them.

4. *Insufficient middle management interest:* This group's participation is vital to establishing and maintaining culture change.

Middle managers often view such attempts as the latest whim of the CEO, or the expensive brainchild of the latest hotshot consultant. If they are to be expected to support changes in the status quo, middle managers must have a rational self-interest in such change.

5. *Too much patience, or too much haste:* Cultural adjustments cannot be completed overnight, but they are not generational events either. The organization should establish how much movement is required—changing a product-driven organization into a distribution-driven organization is a greater leap than moving from product to technology, for example—and then determine a reasonable time frame to effect the change.

6. *Inappropriate expectations:* Employees expecting too much or too little, too soon or too late, is really a result of poor participation and a lack of "ownership." Management should keep everyone apprised of what to expect and what the ramifications will be. For instance, an organization placing new emphasis on customer service responsiveness might also place more emphasis on performance evaluation: speed of response, accuracy of response, number of complaints, and so on. Ideally, this organization would let everyone know that new evaluation procedures will be implemented in three months, that standards will be set between employee and supervisor, and that 20 percent of everyone's bonus will ride on the evaluation. "Any questions? Let us know in the next thirty days."

The elements of a productive, constructive culture could be summarized in this manner:

I. *People*
- Appropriate traits and characteristics—can-do
- Appropriate behaviors and motivation—want-to-do
- Identification with job and its role—should-do

II. *Teamwork*
- Independence of the team to act—perceived power
- Shared understanding of goals—absence of conflict over goals
- Agreement on methods—absence of conflict over how to achieve goals
- Trust in each other—minimum of bureaucratic procedures
- Reinforcement and support—perceived backing of superiors

III. *Structure*

- Systems and procedures are clear and unobstructive
- Techniques are available to resolve ambiguity
- Coordination with and contribution to other functions are both clear
- Individual, team, and organization objectives are in harmony
- "Freedom to fail" is real

IV. *Leadership*

- Supportive
- Participative
- Results-oriented not activity-oriented
- Flexible
- Maintains links with other units and superiors
- Protects and defends if necessary

V. *Senior Management*

- Focus on productivity, not activity
- Exemplifies values consistently
- Rewards results objectively
- Communicates honestly
- Establishes goals that are relevant to employees
- Provides appropriate resources
- Establishes strategic directions

Cultural Frameworks

Words like "culture," "values," "ethics," "beliefs," and "integrity" have become the buzzwords in business (and business schools) only recently. Yet longtime successful organizations have always made these concepts an intrinsic aspect of what their enterprise is all about. Here is one way to visualize the relationships between corporate beliefs and values and corporate organizations and performance.[4]

Corporate beliefs and values are those core beliefs that drive the organization, influence its nature and direction, and help determine strategy. Such corporate beliefs may be:

- Strive to be the perceived and actual leaders in information technology
- Apply the latest scientific findings to areas of human need

- Provide unexcelled service for the business traveler
- Attain maximum profit per passenger mile
- Gain additional market share every year
- Aim toward being named number one in our field by independent polls.

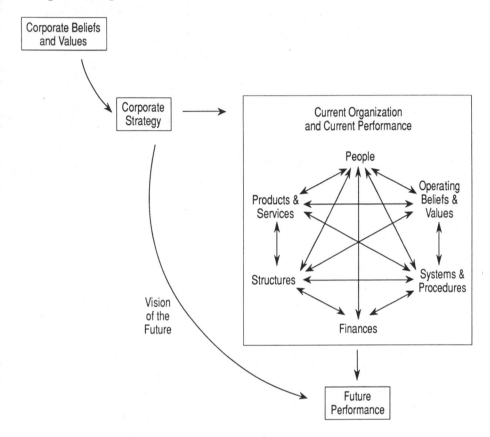

Such corporate values will help determine the strategy that will in turn create the plans and operating guidelines required not only for the organization to perform today, but also for it to reach the performance goals called for by the strategy. The various factors cited in the Current Organization and Current Performance box must be actively managed to make the future vision into a reality. This is where cultural change is often required—because the organization and its people "can't get there from here" by simply doing more of what they're currently doing. Some things must be done differently, or better, or not at all, and some new policies and procedures most likely will have to be added.

The *operating* beliefs and values within the Current Organization and Current Performance box are those that employees utilize on a daily basis. These beliefs must be consistent with (or, at least, not in opposition to) the corporate beliefs. Few employees bear in mind each day that they should be attaining the maximum profit per passenger mile, or gaining additional market share each year. One bank president recognizes this fact: "I know my branch managers aren't focused on increasing shareholder value each time they make a decision. My job is to ensure that what they *are* focused on—retaining IRA accounts, attracting refinancing business, luring commercial accounts, whatever—*does* increase shareholder value."

Examples of daily operating beliefs and values may include:

- Meet our monthly quotas
- Support the field force
- Provide patient and responsive customer service
- Be accurate in all financial reporting
- Conform carefully to legal requirements
- Pay claims within two working days
- Do the right thing for the customer

The last is not lip service. It's the most prevalent core belief for all levels of managers at one of our clients, Merck & Co., which we cited earlier for being America's most admired company in *Fortune* magazine's poll of CEOs. Merck managers constantly ask, "What is best for the patient and the physician?" when deciding on product information, call frequency, and priorities.

But we've painted the positive picture. In many organizations, the operating values and beliefs are:

- Cover your rear
- Avoid criticism
- Make your quotas, even at the sacrifice of quality
- Don't trust management
- Never volunteer and always look busy
- Don't do too well or you'll get all the work
- Always ask, "What's in it for me?"

How does an organization—how do managers—"move" employees to positive beliefs that are consistent with corporate beliefs and goals? In the first place, "movement" isn't what we want— it's motivation that's the key. While helping employees to motivate themselves—especially in the direction the organization seeks to go—is easier said than done, there are some reliable approaches to accomplishing this. You'll note that these approaches synthesize issues covered in the prior chapters—power, trust, selection, and the like—and that none of them purport to be a miracle cure. Organizational culture isn't changed on the side of a mountain, in a river raft, or over hot coals. It's changed *on the job*—in the environment in which the culture operates.

Here are some suggestions then, for the successful management of corporate culture. These guidelines should allow the individual and the organization to self-actualize and scale the hierarchy of needs that Maslow described.

Support your employees by:

1. Selecting people with the right capabilities *and* behaviors
2. Providing autonomy and freedom from excessive controls
3. Demonstrating trust that employees' skills, knowledge, and judgment are appropriate
4. Providing requisite resources
5. Providing consistent, reliable, and predictable leadership
6. Communicating clearly, honestly, and frequently
7. Exemplifying the behaviors and values you wish to establish

Change or strengthen your corporate culture by:

1. Sharing with employees the overall corporate mission frequently
2. Aligning the operating beliefs with the corporate beliefs
3. Creating a participative management style
4. Focusing on results and rewarding results
5. Encouraging teams to set standards and goals
6. Appealing to self-interest to enhance motivation
7. Adjusting values and goals as the business environment changes
8. Making the CEO an active, visible adherent of the desired values
9. Maintaining values in concise, simple terms
10. Testing your progress by assessing how people are investing their time, energy, and reputations

In many organizations, the culture is a loose cannon. It is influenced by external conditions, societal mores, competition, employee beliefs, fads, even external consultants. No less than financial resources, customers, patents, trade secrets, and R&D,

organizational culture should be consciously and proactively managed according to corporate beliefs and corporate strategy. To do any less is to disconnect the rudder and wonder why the ship doesn't respond to the helm.

Environmental Trends

We've spoken several times of the "environment." One of the reasons the environment is so important, for both individual and organizational success, is that it provides clues about the future. And those clues are very important in determining the kinds of skills, behaviors, and cultures that will be required for future success. No successful organization should be hiring and training today for *today's* needs. It should be acting today on *tomorrow's* needs. When the role of mortgage loan originator changed owing to the deregulation of banking and dramatically increased competition, the leading-edge banks had already begun hiring and training a new kind of loan originator—a more sales-oriented person with a high level of persuasiveness and a higher tolerance for ambiguity. But even today, we still find some banks hiring old-style loan originators with high attention to detail, high levels of patience, and low people orientation—as though they will still be sitting in an office accepting or rejecting loan applications from people who had nowhere else to go!

Here, then, is one assessment of significant trends that should substantially influence people and their work in the years ahead. The failure to anticipate these and other trends could send people and organizations scurrying *down* Maslow's hierarchy.

1. Valuing Human Resources as a Key Lever for Raising Productivity. We are in an age of great emphasis on productivity. In view of scarce resources, increasing international competition, decreasing U.S. population growth, and cutbacks of public-sector services, it is likely that this emphasis will continue throughout the remainder of this century.

But productivity is one of those concepts that is easier to understand than to attain. There are some productivity gains to be achieved through advances in automation, robotics, and computerization. But the most profound advances will come from an organization's *human* resources—its people. There is insufficient capital and insufficient incentive to rebuild the steel mills and plants of other manufacturing industries. But there are gains to be made from the people running the mills and the support services nurturing them. And as our economy becomes increasingly service- and knowledge-based, productivity advances will be a result primarily of people and their relationship to work.

Managers will become involved in what may be termed "holistic humanism," meaning, an approach that considers the whole person and the entirety of his or her learning and development needs. Managers will be responsible for bringing the power of the organization to bear on these issues. Conversely, the abilities of individuals must be focused on the pressures affecting the organization.

2. The Computer Revolution. This term is something of a misnomer. We are really experiencing a microprocessor revolution. Computers have been with us since the late 1940s. But the miniaturization of the microprocessor has enabled the computer to become a daily companion and an easily accessible tool. And unlike so many other breakthroughs that rely on expensive, rare materials, the basis for this revolution is the extraordinarly abundant raw material, silica.

A large burden will fall on human resource (HR) professionals to provide training in the use of the computer to assist in decision making, projecting alternative futures based on various options, assessing risk, and—most importantly—deciding when *not* to utilize the computer. Moreover, the computer's potential for having a dehumanizing effect in the workplace is fairly high. There will also be an increased need for attitudinal training to handle the isolation inherent in many computer operations.

The computer revolution will radically alter the way in which people learn, in some cases changing the venue of the learning itself. And coupled with the third trend, it will transform our lives.

3. Adult Education and the Lifelong Learner. The quality of life remains a key concern of an increasingly sophisticated work force. Education enhances the quality of life and it will be provided in larger and larger measures by the employer—as a very cost-effective employee benefit—and will not be restricted to job-related skills.

The combination of the enhanced learning made possible by the computer revolution and the greater need for and receptivity to learning created by the adult learner market will have an enormous impact on everyone concerned with managing people. Education, training, career development, and other areas are going to lose their separate identities and will become parts of an integrated, comprehensive system of personal and professional growth.

4. The Increasing Internationalization of Business. For the first time in business history, international management is becoming a major factor in the operations of the organization. More U.S. firms than ever before are doing business in other countries, and more overseas firms than ever before are doing business in the United States. Moreover, these firms are not just the traditional multinational giants. Small and medium-sized businesses are being pulled into the international arena as well.

Managers at a variety of levels in an organization will be called upon to deal with a mix of different cultures, sometimes even as part of a single business venture. They might be required to buy from the Germans, sell to the French, and compete with the Dutch. Although cultural training is in its infancy, courses such as "How to Negotiate with the Japanese" are usually sold out as soon as they are offered. Such delicate dealings were once handled by only the most senior management. Today, managers far down the corporate ladder must deal with these sensitive relationships, too.

5. The Transformation of the Work Force from Manufacturing Workers to Knowledge Workers. The term "knowledge worker" has been defined in a variety of ways. Basically, it refers to a worker whose entire job is the accumulation, transfer, validation, analysis, and creation of information. The airlines reservation agent, seated at a computer terminal with a telephone headset for virtually the entire workday, is a knowledge worker. Teachers and telephone operators are traditional knowledge workers. But so, too, are legions of insurance company employees, stockbrokers, newspeople, and air traffic controllers. More and more people—even within traditional manufacturing concerns—are dealing exclusively with data and information rather than with the production of a product or a physical service.

Two allied developments have accelerated this often discussed phenomenon. One is the computer and its impact on data handling.[5] The other is the erosion of our manufacturing sector.

The primary American industries of twenty years ago were steel, automobiles, oil, rubber, textiles, paper, and the like. Today, the up-and-coming industries include computers and peripherals, diversified financial, entertainment, and sports, and so forth. There has been a massive shift in our economic base from manufacturing toward service and knowledge.

The fact is that there will be tremendous need to retrain workers—in both skills and attitudes—but this should be done without massive uprootings. (An analogous effort was required to incorporate automation into the workplace in the 1950s.) For example, if we look at one of the most traditional of American Industries—the paper industry—we find that the people required to run and maintain a paper machine through its three-shift workday have changed in number and function. The machines today are computerized. Workers read control panels and write-outs instead of listening for the odd thump in the machinery or spotting oil leaks. By and large, however, the same people are working on the machine today as twenty years ago. In an increasingly sophisticated age, they have adapted to an increasingly sophisticated job. But they must be managed much differently—not on the basis of their *content* knowledge, but as part of the *team*.

6. *The Increasing Sophistication of Training and Development Programs and Increasing Wariness of Fads.* The actor Burt Reynolds once noted that the life cycle of a star was summed up in this sequence:

"Who's Burt Reynolds?"
"Get me that Burt Reynolds guy."
"Can we get Burt Reynolds?"
"Can we get a Burt Reynolds type?"
"Get me a young Burt Reynolds."
"Who's Burt Reynolds?"

Unfortunately, fads in management development are not much different. Transactional analysis (TA) comes to mind as an approach that was once on everyone's lips (and in everyone's budget?) and is now almost never discussed. The truth is that TA has some very valid aspects and is very useful in certain situations for addressing certain needs. Unhappily, both its utility and impact were overstated as the bandwagon roared down the hill. Perhaps it will return in a revised form that will enable us to keep the proper perspective on it. Quality control circles are a more recent embodiment of the search for the magic training pill.

Training and development, as a profession, has suffered from a lack of respectability. There are no truly effective boards or examinations to certify one as a consultant or trainer. Professional associations in the field are forced to be either all things to all people (like the American Society for Training and Development, or the American Management Association) or highly specialized and small (the Instructional Systems Association). Many blue-collar fields require much more stringent qualifications. Indeed, it is all too easy to hang out a consultant's shingle.

Conversely, it has become more difficult to become a *buyer* of management development services. Pressures on the budget—for results and from competitors—have combined to make the buyer much more selective. In addition, it is no longer unusual to find a specialist sitting in the HR seat whose academic background, organizational assignments, and professional affiliations justly qualify him or her as a legitimate in-house professional. In other words, a combination of pressures and the recognition of HR's importance to the long-term health of the organization has created a buyer who might be more qualified than the seller.

Most serious HR professionals are realizing that the most efficacious development of people occurs when they are shown what they already do well and are helped to repeat those skills as often as possible. Imposing new systems and behaviors on people just doesn't work, no matter how impressive the author or colorful the package. Training has become subject to the same kind of return-on-investment scrutiny that other organizational efforts are subject to, and this trend will certainly continue.

7. *The Interdependence of the Public and Private Sectors.* Managers are being called on more than ever before to deal with both sectors of the economy. Government regulation, multinational business dealings, and "corporate citizenship" are among the reasons for this emphasis. However, there is often a culture shock for the manager used to working in one sector who begins to work in the other. Timing, the nature of decision making, budget provisions, pluralism, and varying constituencies all combine to differentiate the two areas.

However, there is also the trend among not-for-profit organizations of every type to embrace the management style of profit-oriented organizations. "Administrators" feel free to call themselves "managers" today without feeling soiled by the effort. Moreover, nonperformers are no longer tolerated just because they serve in a "good cause."[6] Responsibility for the bottom line, productivity, and organizational effectiveness have turned out to be areas where nonprofits admit they can learn from the private sector. More sophisticated, goal-oriented management techniques are needed.

"Third sector" organizations—schools, hospitals, community groups, foundations, museums, churches, social organizations, professional partnerships—will face more, not less, challenge in the 1990s. While they all have some unique needs, they also must deal with the management of people, money, and the market.

Among these challenges will be

- Professional scientists, chemists, doctors, and others who find themselves in management positions will need a new set of skills, separate from their previous professional training. This will be a most sophisticated, mature, and perhaps difficult group of learners.

- Training and education will have to be individualized, tailored, and modularized to the time demands and work habits of such people and institutions.

- "Cultural" training will be required to assist public- or private-sector managers at all levels to deal with each other and with each other's environments.

8. The Symbiotic Relationships. Many industries thrive by relying heavily on independent businesses. Pharmaceutical companies rely on independent laboratories, airlines on travel agents, soda manuafacturers on bottlers, and fast-food organizations on their franchise holders. In the past, many "parent" organizations wined and dined those upon whom they were dependent. However, food and drink will soon take a backseat to education more often than not.

How much more effctive is it for an airline to provide basic business education to independent travel agents? Such an approach makes the agents better businesspeople—which is vital to the success of both the agents and the airline—and also places the airline in a favorable light. Anyone with a checkbook can wine and dine, but how many organizations have the maturity and farsightedness to provide an educational experience that otherwise would never have occurred?

Such synergy will increase dramatically. Banks, now in a highly competitive position, will offer management education to their clients for a variety of reasons, including (1) wanting their customers to manage their businesses and the bank's money well, and (2) knowing that the competition to lend the funds is going to demand such ancillary services.

This has not been intended to be an exhaustive analysis of the business environment, nor a futurist's prediction of the next ten years. Rather, experience indicates that these are the pressures that are beginning to be felt today, and there is reasonable evidence that they will exert a major influence on managerial and organizational performance.

What is the prescription for managers that will enable them to reconcile these pressures and create the synergy necessary for the decade ahead? Here are the components for a new, holistic approach to managing people:

1. Take a strategic as well as operational view of human resource needs. Determine what the philosophy and basic beliefs of the function are and should be for your organization. Don't measure yourself solely by the quality (or worse,

quantity) of what you provide, but rather, evaluate how well you have anticipated needs and developed resources to meet these needs.

2. Help train others to think and act strategically. There are no sure answers in strategic thinking. Take the lead in exploring alternatives and disseminating information on how the firm can tackle its strategic issues.

3. Specify the HR role within the overall strategy of the organization. Top management will have two major concerns: products and markets, and people. HR is fully half of that combination. Become cognizant of the company's strategy, and proactively support the HR role within it.

4. Stay abreast of general business developments. Become familiar with areas even peripherally affecting your industry. Hone your financial skills. Learn more about international business issues.

Toward Better Management

Our contention has been that, of three primary job components, behavior is often ignored, misunderstood, or abused by managers. This is not the result of a malicious disregard for the role of managing and motivating people, but simply the product of systems, procedures, and inertia from another age.

In "days of yore," managers were repositories of information, and they controlled and directed according to their personal content knowledge of their jobs. After all, managers had commonly performed every job for which they became responsible, having risen through a military-like hierarchy by seniority. In a relatively unchanging world, their goals were to protect their position, preserve the status quo, and avoid disruptions until additional seniority dictated another promotion.

Things are somewhat different today. We've come from the age of the brontosaurus to the age of the cheetah.

Today, virtually everyone has instantaneous access to data—it isn't parcelled out by "those in the know," not with a computer sitting on everyone's desk. And the focus these days is not on content, but on processes—managing marketing processes, financial processes, and communications processes. It's neither who you know nor what you know, but how well you understand the world around you that matters.

That world is composed of people: subordinates, peers, superiors, customers, vendors, competitors, regulators, stockholders, prospects, and others. The great performance breakthroughs to be achieved by computerization, automation, miniaturization, decentralization, and so on have largely been made. The great potential—perhaps unlimited potential—for continuing performance improvement is in the people area. And the people area that is least understood and utilized by management is that of behavioral compatibility.

Here's a checklist for adding the techniques we've presented in this book to your management repertoire. Some may not apply at the moment, but all should be reviewed periodically to ensure that you're doing all you can to effectively manage and influence others:

- Determine behavioral requirements of jobs and incorporate them into position descriptions.
- Measure and assess individual behaviors and compare them to job demands.
- Provide job modifications, job aids, and/or external assistance when there is a less than perfect match between the job demands and the performer's behavior.
- Change the jobs of those whose behavior is poorly suited to their job—don't throw training or motivation at a behavioral mismatch.
- Determine those behaviors that others are most receptive to and modify your behaviors accordingly when you wish to influence those people.
- Determine and act on the behavioral underpinnings of conflicts, confrontations, bureaucratic inertia, and lack of trust—don't simply apply a label or a stereotype and assume you must live with the problem.
- Help others to change their behavior by assisting them in understanding why they act the way they do and how to modify their actions.
- Prevent stress—one of the greatest detriments to performance—by using the preceding items on a daily basis with your subordinates and colleagues.

We introduced this book by stressing the importance of people, positions, and performance. These three factors are at the heart of motivated, self-perpetuating high performance—for individuals and for organizations. Behavior is the common denominator for all three factors: The positions must be understood in terms of the behavioral demands they entail. (Toll collection requires high consistency, architecture high attention to detail.) The person must be evaluated in terms of how well his or her behavioral predispositions match the job demands. (Bill will need an assistant to handle the details; Maria will need to reduce her socializing.) The ensuing performance must be reinforced and rewarded to create optimal behavioral compatibility. (Joan's best when things are consistent—let's not keep changing her staff around; Larry's "big picture" thinking is ideal for the strategy project.)

Management isn't becoming more sophisticated, despite what many people claim. It *is* becoming more people-oriented, and many organizations tend to deal with people by creating a mechanistic, rule-dominated environment that is *complicated*, not sophisticated. If we can employ a process for dealing successfully with people, despite content, despite the environment, and despite the position in which we find ourselves, we'll be able to manage any organization's most valuable assets consistently and well.

That process is nothing more and nothing less than a behavioral approach to managing and motivating people. As a manager, you'll find that the performance of others is not the result of something the devil made them do. Unless, of course, you're the devil.

Notes

1. Peter Drucker, *The Age of Discontinuity* (New York: Harper & Row, 1968).
2. Peter Drucker, *The Effective Executive* (New York: Harper & Row, 1966).
3. As cited in "Human Resources," *Wall Street Journal*, 17 May 1988, p. 1.
4. The figure on page 159 is adapted from Stanley Davis, *Managing Corporate Culture* (Cambridge, MA: Ballinger Publishing Company, 1984), p. 6.
5. I once heard author and anthropologist Stephen Jay Gould point out that man thought he was the center of the universe, until Copernicus proved otherwise; then he thought he was at least uniquely divine in origin, until Darwin questioned that; then he believed that he was still master of his own will, until Freud raised doubt about that; then he took solace in the fact that his brain, in any event, could uniquely process information; then along came the computer. . . .
6. Peter Drucker, "The Non-Profits' Quiet Revolution," *Wall Street Journal*, 8 September 1988.

Index

About the Author

Alan Weiss is the founder and president of Summit Consulting Group, Inc. His firm specializes in management and organization development and assists over 100 clients in five countries.

An editorial in *Success* magazine has cited Mr. Weiss as a "worldwide expert in trends in executive education." He has published over 200 articles and columns appearing in publications that include the *New York Times, Personnel Journal, Boardroom Reports, Management Review,* and scores of others. Mr. Weiss is a highly sought after speaker who appears regularly at management conferences. He has contributed to two books, *The Handbook of Modern Human Resource Administration* (McGraw-Hill) and *Advocacy Selling: Why Winners Win* (AMACOM). Mr. Weiss and Michel Robert co-authored *The Innovation Formula: How Organizations Turn Change into Opportunity* (Ballinger/Harper & Row).

Mr. Weiss has served as president of Kepner-Tregoe Continuing Education, an international training firm in Princeton, New Jersey, and as president, CEO, and a director of Walter V. Clarke Associates, a behavioral consulting firm in Providence, Rhode Island. In the course of his assignments he has managed domestic and international operations in twenty-three countries. His personal clients include organizations such as Hewlett-Packard, IBM, GTE, Merck & Co., the U.S. Department of Justice, City University of New York, and Marine Midland Bank.

Mr. Weiss resides in East Greenwich, Rhode Island, with his wife, Maria, and their children, Danielle and Jason.